THE KNOWLEDGE OF THE HEBREW BOYS

AKIN AKINYEMI

Syncterface Media
London
www.syncterfacemedia.com

Unless otherwise indicated, all Scripture quotations in this volume are from the King James Version of the Bible. Capitalised text and annotation added for emphasis.

Scripture quotations marked NKJV are taken from the New King James Version of the Bible, quotations marked NIV are from the New International Version and quotations marked AMP are taken from the Amplified Bible, ©1954, 1958, 1962,1964, 1965, 1987 by The Lockman Foundation.
Used by permission.

No part of this book may be reproduced or transmitted in any form or by any means, graphic, electronic, or mechanical, including photocopying, recording, taping or by any information storage or retrieval system, without the permission in writing from the author.

THE KNOWLEDGE OF THE HEBREW BOYS
ISBN: 978-0-9565043-1-9

Copyright.© February 2011 Akin Akinyemi
All Rights Reserved

Published in the United Kingdom by

Syncterface Media
London
www.syncterfacemedia.com
info@syncterfacemedia.com

Cover Design:
Syncterface Media

Contents

Chapter 1: What Knowledge is this? 1
Chapter 2: Knowledge and the gift of word of Knowledge 13
Chapter 3: Qualifying for Knowledge 25
Chapter 4: Operating in Knowledge 59
Chapter 5: The Rewards of Knowledge 81
Chapter 6: Knowledge for Exploits 93
Chapter 7: Demonstrations of Knowledge 103

1

What Knowledge is this?

> ⁶ *My people are destroyed for lack of knowledge: because thou hast rejected knowledge, I will also reject thee, that thou shalt be no priest to me: seeing thou hast forgotten the law of thy God, I will also forget thy children.*
>
> *Hosea 4:6*

The first part of this scripture is a phrase that is well known by almost every believer, a phrase that openly highlights what happens when knowledge is inadequate or missing in the life of a child of God. However, it is the second part of this verse which, though not as familiar, opens our eyes to the importance of this knowledge. It is here that we see that God Himself desires for we His children to get this knowledge, and what happens when we turn our backs on it.

Before we take off on this journey, we need to settle one very vital point. Man was never created to operate completely independent of God. This is extremely crucial as some doctrines of devils being propagated aim to portray man as a god in himself, without his relationship with God. Man can only assume the *God-like* status as a result of words that come from God Himself (*John 10:35*). Anything short of this is falsehood. Jesus never did anything except what He had seen in the Father.

> ³ Now ye are clean through the word which I have spoken unto you.
> ⁴ Abide in me, and I in you. As the branch cannot bear fruit of itself, except it abide in the vine; no more can ye, except ye abide in me.
> ⁵ I am the vine, ye are the branches: He that abideth in me, and I in him, the same bringeth forth much fruit: **FOR WITHOUT ME YE CAN DO NOTHING.**
>
> *John 15:3-5*

We need to understand that though Adam and Eve were both naked or *"bare"* as the literal Hebrew implies, they were not ashamed. This signifies that declaring that we are naked or helpless without God is not a sign of weakness, rather a revelation of a greater relationship that is able to produce superior results. Jesus was quick to respond with this revelation when asked about his identity.

> ²⁵ Then said they unto him, Who art thou? And Jesus saith unto them, Even the same that I said unto you from the beginning.
> ²⁶ I have many things to say and to judge of you: but he that sent me is true; and I speak to the world those things which I have heard of him.
> ²⁷ They understood not that he spake to them of the Father.
> ²⁸ Then said Jesus unto them, When ye have lifted up the Son of man, then shall ye know that I am he, and that I do nothing of myself; but as my Father hath taught me, I speak these things.
> ²⁹ And he that sent me is with me: the Father hath not left me alone; for I do always those things that please him.
>
> *John 8:25-29*

From the very beginning, God was very particular about knowledge. In the Garden of Eden, the one tree God told man not to eat of was the tree of the knowledge of good and evil (*Genesis 2:16-17*). It is quite interesting that prior to eating the fruit, man was not aware that a state of nakedness existed. However, the acquiring of knowledge outside the prescribed order of God showed man his nakedness.

> [6] *And when the woman saw that the tree was good for food, and that it was pleasant to the eyes, and a tree to be desired to make one wise, she took of the fruit thereof, and did eat, and gave also unto her husband with her; and he did eat.*
> [7] *And the eyes of them both were opened, and* **THEY KNEW THAT THEY WERE NAKED**; *and they sewed fig leaves together, and made themselves aprons.*
> [8] *And they heard the voice of the LORD God walking in the garden in the cool of the day: and Adam and his wife hid themselves from the presence of the LORD God amongst the trees of the garden.*
>
> *Genesis 3:6-8*

I wonder what would have happened if Adam had not touched the fruit; would he have been conscious of good and evil? The truth is, knowledge in itself does nothing, but knowledge acted upon is potent. By eating the fruit, a new set of facts presented themselves to Adam, facts that were contrary to the knowledge of God that he already possessed. In Paul's letter to the Corinthian Church, he highlights this contrary knowledge:

> [5] *Casting down imaginations,* **AND EVERY HIGH THING THAT EXALTETH ITSELF AGAINST THE KNOWLEDGE OF GOD**, *and bringing into captivity every thought to the obedience of Christ;*
>
> *2 Corinthians 10:5*

Knowledge usually signifies gaining an awareness of facts, truths, or principles through research, study or some other investigative means. The means of acquiring this knowledge is as important as the knowledge acquired. The book of Proverbs gives us an idea of the kind of searching required to get knowledge:

> ¹ My son, if thou wilt receive my words, and hide my commandments with thee;
> ² So that thou incline thine ear unto wisdom, and apply thine heart to understanding;
> ³ Yea, if thou criest after knowledge, and liftest up thy voice for understanding;
> ⁴ If thou seekest her as silver, and searchest for her as for hid treasures;
> ⁵ Then shalt thou understand the fear of the LORD, and find the knowledge of God.
> ⁶ For the LORD giveth wisdom: out of his mouth cometh knowledge and understanding.
>
> *Proverbs 2:1-6*

Knowledge determines the degree to which you can control your thoughts and the boundaries to which your imagination can be flexed. While memories deal with the past, and cannot be changed, thoughts deal with the present and are framed by knowledge. Imagination on the other hand deals with the future. Imagination is the thought of future possibilities based on current knowledge. If the knowledge you have makes you realise that you are naked, life will be a burden and just like Adam, when you hear the voice of limitless possibilities you will run away and hide.

So, if having this knowledge is so crucial it then becomes imperative for every believer to know its source and to understand it. So, the big question is, *"what exactly is this knowledge?"*

What is Knowledge?

To understand this knowledge in a bit more detail let us take a brief look at the experience of *Daniel, Shadrach, Meshach* and *Abednego*; the Hebrew boys!

> ³ And the king spake unto Ashpenaz the master of his eunuchs, that

What Knowledge is this?

he should bring certain of the children of Israel, and of the king's seed, and of the princes;

4 CHILDREN IN WHOM WAS NO BLEMISH, BUT WELL FAVOURED, AND SKILFUL IN ALL WISDOM, AND CUNNING IN KNOWLEDGE, AND UNDERSTANDING SCIENCE, AND SUCH AS HAD ABILITY IN THEM TO STAND IN THE KING'S PALACE, AND WHOM THEY MIGHT TEACH THE LEARNING AND THE TONGUE OF THE CHALDEANS.

⁵ And the king appointed them a daily provision of the king's meat, and of the wine which he drank: so nourishing them three years, that at the end thereof they might stand before the king.

⁶ Now among these were of the children of Judah, Daniel, Hananiah, Mishael, and Azariah:

⁷ Unto whom the prince of the eunuchs gave names: for he gave unto Daniel the name of Belteshazzar; and to Hananiah, of Shadrach; and to Mishael, of Meshach; and to Azariah, of Abednego.

⁸ But Daniel purposed in his heart that he would not defile himself with the portion of the king's meat, nor with the wine which he drank: therefore he requested of the prince of the eunuchs that he might not defile himself.

⁹ Now God had brought Daniel into favour and tender love with the prince of the eunuchs.

¹⁰ And the prince of the eunuchs said unto Daniel, I fear my lord the king, who hath appointed your meat and your drink: for why should he see your faces worse liking than the children which are of your sort? then shall ye make me endanger my head to the king.

¹¹ Then said Daniel to Melzar, whom the prince of the eunuchs had set over Daniel, Hananiah, Mishael, and Azariah,

¹² Prove thy servants, I beseech thee, ten days; and let them give us pulse to eat, and water to drink.

¹³ Then let our countenances be looked upon before thee, and the countenance of the children that eat of the portion of the king's meat: and as thou seest, deal with thy servants.

¹⁴ So he consented to them in this matter, and proved them ten days.

¹⁵ And at the end of ten days their countenances appeared fairer and fatter in flesh than all the children which did eat the portion of the king's meat.

¹⁶ Thus Melzar took away the portion of their meat, and the wine that they should drink; and gave them pulse.

¹⁷ As for these four children, **GOD GAVE THEM KNOWLEDGE** and skill in all learning and wisdom: and Daniel had understanding in

all visions and dreams.
¹⁸ Now at the end of the days that the king had said he should bring them in, then the prince of the eunuchs brought them in before Nebuchadnezzar.
¹⁹ And the king communed with them; and among them all was found none like Daniel, Hananiah, Mishael, and Azariah: therefore stood they before the king.
²⁰ And in all matters of wisdom and understanding, that the king enquired of them, he found them ten times better than all the magicians and astrologers that were in all his realm.

Daniel 1:3-20

Knowledge: Being abreast of facts

In the biblical context, the word *"knowledge"*, which appears almost two hundred times in the Old Testament, has different meanings each of which could considerably alter the context in which the word is rendered.

The Hebrew boys were given knowledge by God (*Daniel 1:17*), but they did not suddenly know everything about subjects they had not studied. In *Daniel 1:4*, following the defeat of Judah, we see that the king of Babylon was looking for children who were *"skilful in all wisdom, cunning in knowledge, who understood science"* so they could be taught the learning and the tongue of the Chaldeans.

While this request seems rather simple, a closer look into the Hebrew word translated knowledge here provides a lot more insight into the king's request. The root word {da'ath} implies *"awareness and not being ignorant of facts"*. Nebuchad-nez'-zar, the king of Babylon, was looking for people with the ability to use facts as is done in a judicial system.

Under normal legal circumstances, if a prosecutor does not have enough evidence, a guilty defendant could walk free. With the emergence of new technology in DNA analysis in recent years, prosecutors with new facts on a case can reopen cases and people who had previously been freed can be convicted. The ability of an individual to use facts skilfully could mean the difference between guilty and not guilty. We see the importance of facts when the Psalmist says:

> [10] *He that chastiseth the heathen, shall not he correct?* **HE THAT TEACHETH MAN KNOWLEDGE, SHALL NOT HE KNOW?.**
>
> *Psalm 94:10*

One of the greatest demonstrations of facts we see in the Bible was that of Stephen, when he was giving a speech to the council in *Acts 7:1-53*. Stephen talked with great accuracy and undeniable facts from Abraham to Solomon covering hundreds of years of history.

I remember looking into the story of one of the most successful Management Consulting firms around and found that one of the factors that differentiated them from the others was the aggressive nature with which they went after facts while on engagements with clients. This drive for facts always compensated for the lack of understanding any new recruit may have about the sector in which they were going to be working.

The absence of this type of knowledge brings captivity. Both Old Testament prophets Isaiah and Hosea used this same Hebrew word to refer to knowledge in *Isaiah 5:13* and *Hosea 4:6*.

> [13] *Therefore My people go into captivity [to their enemies] without knowing it and because they have no* **KNOWLEDGE** *[of God]. And their honorable men [their glory] are famished, and their common people are parched with thirst.*
>
> *Isaiah 5:13 (AMP)*

> *⁶ My people are destroyed for lack of **KNOWLEDGE**; because you [the priestly nation] have rejected **KNOWLEDGE**, I will also reject you that you shall be no priest to Me; seeing you have forgotten the law of your God, I will also forget your children.*
>
> Hosea 4:6 (AMP)

Facts are the part of knowledge that the world can relate to. It provides the evidence of the ability (*the truth of the Word of God*) within.

Knowledge: Possessing ability

The knowledge God gave to the Hebrew boys was different from the one that keeps you abreast of facts. It implies *"the ability, intelligence or consciousness of mind to acquire and comprehend facts, truths and principles through observation, recognition and intuition by the application of care and diligence"*

Putting this definition of knowledge in *Daniel 1:17*, we see a higher order of knowledge. God's gift to the Hebrew boys was not merely facts, it was a lot greater:

> *¹⁷ As for these four children, God gave them knowledge (**THE ABILITY, INTELLIGENCE OR CONSCIOUSNESS OF MIND TO ACQUIRE AND COMPREHEND FACTS, TRUTHS AND PRINCIPLES THROUGH OBSERVATION, RECOGNITION AND INTUITION BY THE APPLICATION OF CARE AND DILIGENCE**) and skill in all learning and wisdom: and Daniel had understanding in all visions and dreams.*
>
> Daniel 1:17

This was the same type of knowledge that Solomon asked for when his kingdom was being established:

> *⁷ In that night did God appear unto Solomon, and said unto him, Ask what I shall give thee.*
> *⁸ And Solomon said unto God, Thou hast shewed great mercy unto David my father, and hast made me to reign in his stead.*
> *⁹ Now, O LORD God, let thy promise unto David my father be established: for thou hast made me king over a people like the dust of*

> the earth in multitude.
> ¹⁰ GIVE ME NOW WISDOM AND KNOWLEDGE, that I may go out and come in before this people: for who can judge this thy people, that is so great?
> ¹¹ And God said to Solomon, Because this was in thine heart, and thou hast not asked riches, wealth, or honour, nor the life of thine enemies, neither yet hast asked long life; but hast asked wisdom and knowledge for thyself, that thou mayest judge my people, over whom I have made thee king:
> ¹² WISDOM AND KNOWLEDGE IS GRANTED UNTO THEE; and I will give thee riches, and wealth, and honour, such as none of the kings have had that have been before thee, neither shall there any after thee have the like.
>
> 2 Chronicles 1:7-12

God granted Solomon this knowledge and as a result he had a largeness and depth of heart that gave him the ability to process different courses of action in the affairs of life accurately. *1 Kings 3:16-27* shows the wisdom and knowledge Solomon got in action. After seeing and hearing of this manifestation of this gift of God, the people feared the king. I believe that one reason a lot of people, particularly in western countries, despise the gospel is because believers are not manifesting their gifts.

> ²⁸ And all Israel heard of the judgment which the king had judged; and they feared the king: for they saw that the wisdom of God was in him, to do judgment.
>
> 1 Kings 3:28

Unfortunately, too many believers are not obtaining results through faith but through the adoption of principles of the world. We want *"a saul"* to be king over us like the nations of the world but the world is waiting for the manifestation of the sons of God that they may fall down and worship Him. Let us arise and not reject this knowledge.

As believers we cannot operate effectively without both

types of knowledge. Look at the story of Jacob. His compensation was based on the number of spotted and speckled cattle, brown sheep and spotted and speckled goats.

I have noticed something in a lot of Christians today. We usually want to be rewarded based on potential and not on results. Great achievers deliver great results while developing their potential. Jacob's results were not based on perceived potential, they were based on actual results. Any cattle or goat that delivered spotted and speckled offspring belonged to Jacob and any brown cattle or goat belonged to Laban.

> *^{31} And he said, What shall I give thee? And Jacob said, Thou shalt not give me any thing: if thou wilt do this thing for me, I will again feed and keep thy flock.*
> *^{32} I will pass through all thy flock to day, removing from thence all the speckled and spotted cattle, and all the brown cattle among the sheep, and the spotted and speckled among the goats: and of such shall be my hire.*
> *^{33} So shall my righteousness answer for me in time to come, when it shall come for my hire before thy face: every one that is not speckled and spotted among the goats, and brown among the sheep, that shall be counted stolen with me.*
> *^{34} And Laban said, Behold, I would it might be according to thy word.*
> *^{35} And he removed that day the he goats that were ringstraked and spotted, and all the she goats that were speckled and spotted, and every one that had some white in it, and all the brown among the sheep, and gave them into the hand of his sons.*
>
> *Genesis 30:31-35*

Have you ever wondered how Jacob knew what to do to make his spotted cattle, brown sheep and spotted and speckled goat give birth to stronger young?

Chapter Key Points

Knowledge in itself does nothing, but knowledge acted upon is potent

The means of acquiring this knowledge is as important as the knowledge acquired

Knowledge determines the degree to which you can control your thoughts and the boundaries to which your imagination can be flexed

Imagination is the thought of future possibilities based on current knowledge

If the knowledge you have makes you realise that you are naked, life will be a burden and just like Adam, when you hear the voice of limitless possibilities you will run away and hide

2

Knowledge and the gift of word of Knowledge

From the story of the Hebrew boys, we realise that the knowledge they had was a gift from God as stated in *Daniel 1:17*. While the source of this knowledge was God, we now know that the knowledge these boys had was an ability and that the boys took certain actions that gave the ability the opportunity to produce results. The knowledge we are talking about here goes beyond just knowing without results, it reaches the point of being productive in the real issues of life. For example, Daniel spent time studying so he could find answers to the questions of the time;

> ² *In the first year of his reign* **I DANIEL UNDERSTOOD BY BOOKS** *the number of the years, whereof the word of the LORD came to Jeremiah the prophet...*
>
> *Daniel 9:2*

Though the knowledge God gave the Hebrew boys was the ability to assimilate and comprehend facts, they still had to be presented with the materials or situations to be studied. It was not as though a lightning bolt hit them and suddenly they understood all that there was to be understood about the learning and the tongue of the Chaldeans (*generally believed to be present day Iraq*). It took three years of study. As in the case of a pregnant woman, in which the act of conception is not the same as that of delivery, so it is in spiritual things. A lot of people confuse conception (*revelation entering the heart*) and delivery (*revelation bringing forth physical manifestation*) in the things of the kingdom. The things of God usually come as a seed (*James 1:18, 1 Peter 2:23*), which if nurtured, develop into the expectation that prompted God to plant this seed in the heart in the first place.

> ⁵ And the king appointed them a daily provision of the king's meat, and of the wine which he drank: SO NOURISHING THEM THREE YEARS, that at the end thereof they might stand before the king
>
> Daniel 1:5

At the end of three years of nurturing this supernatural ability, these Hebrew boys were not merely ten times better than the regular men of the time. They were ten times better than the magicians. This is quite significant as in the old Testament times, the king usually turned to magicians and wise men, that is, people with supernatural ability, in times of need as was the case in the story of Moses and Pharaoh in Exodus and the story of birth of Jesus and Herod in the gospels.

> ¹⁷ As for these four children, God gave them knowledge and skill in all learning and wisdom: and Daniel had understanding in all visions and dreams.
> ¹⁸ Now at the end of the days that the king had said he should bring them in, then the prince of the eunuchs brought them in before Nebuchadnezzar.
> ¹⁹ And the king communed with them; and among them all was found

none like Daniel, Hananiah, Mishael, and Azariah: therefore stood they before the king.
20 AND IN ALL MATTERS OF WISDOM AND UNDERSTANDING, THAT THE KING ENQUIRED OF THEM, HE FOUND THEM TEN TIMES BETTER THAN ALL THE MAGICIANS AND ASTROLOGERS THAT WERE IN ALL HIS REALM.

Daniel 1:17-22

The knowledge the Hebrew boys had was far superior to the demonic powers at work in the magicians. The supernatural ability from God was superior and this is still the case today. True knowledge starts in God. He was in the beginning of all things. Before man began, God was. (*Genesis 1:1*) If we want to understand this true knowledge, going back to the person who existed in the beginning should be a good starting point. Read what the writer of Proverbs had to say.

[22] *The LORD possessed me in the beginning of his way, before his works of old.*
[23] *I was set up from everlasting, from the beginning, or ever the earth was.*
[24] *When there were no depths, I was brought forth; when there were no fountains abounding with water.*
[25] *Before the mountains were settled, before the hills was I brought forth:*
[26] *While as yet he had not made the earth, nor the fields, nor the highest part of the dust of the world.*
[27] *When he prepared the heavens, I was there: when he set a compass upon the face of the depth:*
[28] *When he established the clouds above: when he strengthened the fountains of the deep:*
[29] *When he gave to the sea his decree, that the waters should not pass his commandment: when he appointed the foundations of the earth:*
[30] *Then I was by him, as one brought up with him: and I was daily his delight, rejoicing always before him;*
[31] *Rejoicing in the habitable part of his earth; and my delights were with the sons of men.*
[32] *Now therefore hearken unto me, O ye children: for blessed are they*

that keep my ways.
³³ Hear instruction, and be wise, and refuse it not.

Proverbs 8:22-33

The fear of the Lord is the beginning of this knowledge. Without God, there is no knowledge. He is the author of knowledge and the fountain of inspiration.

³ Yea, if thou criest after knowledge, and liftest up thy voice for understanding;
⁴ If thou seekest her as silver, and searchest for her as for hid treasures;
*⁵ **THEN SHALT THOU UNDERSTAND THE FEAR OF THE LORD, AND FIND THE KNOWLEDGE OF GOD.***
⁶ For the LORD giveth wisdom: out of his mouth cometh knowledge and understanding.

Proverbs 2:3-6

Having knowledge without God can only get you so far. It is as a branch cut from a tree that loses its source of sustenance. Any branch cut from a tree always falls downward. It never goes up. In like manner, anyone cut-off from God always goes down and falls short of glory (*Romans 3:23*). Is it possible to have a gift that reveals things? Is it possible to know things you have not studied? Well, there is a gift of the spirit called the *"Word of Knowledge"*

The Word of Knowledge

Apostle Paul in his letter to the church at Corinth lists a number of gifts of the Holy Spirit. One of these is called the gift of *"Word of Knowledge"*.

¹ Now concerning spiritual gifts, brethren, I would not have you ignorant.
² Ye know that ye were Gentiles, carried away unto these dumb idols, even as ye were led.
³ Wherefore I give you to understand, that no man speaking by the Spirit of God calleth Jesus accursed: and that no man can say that

Knowledge and the gift of word of Knowledge

Jesus is the Lord, but by the Holy Ghost.
⁴ Now there are diversities of gifts, but the same Spirit.
⁵ And there are differences of administrations, but the same Lord.
⁶ And there are diversities of operations, but it is the same God which worketh all in all.
⁷ But the manifestation of the Spirit is given to every man to profit withal.
⁸ For to one is given by the Spirit the word of wisdom; to another **THE WORD OF KNOWLEDGE** by the same Spirit;
⁹ To another faith by the same Spirit; to another the gifts of healing by the same Spirit;
¹⁰ To another the working of miracles; to another prophecy; to another discerning of spirits; to another divers kinds of tongues; to another the interpretation of tongues:
¹¹ But all these worketh that one and the selfsame Spirit, dividing to every man severally as he will.

1 Corinthians 12:1-12

Notice that this does not say the gift of knowledge, it says the gift of *"word of knowledge"*. What does this mean? The *greek* word used for *"word"* is *"{logos}"* which implies *a spoken word - including the thought or reasoning* - revealing motive or intentions concerning a subject of which the speaker had no prior knowledge.

The sort of thought or reasoning referred to here is not as a result of the mental faculties of the speaker. The believer cannot read a book or some other material then say they have the word of knowledge, particularly if any one that accesses the same book or material will gain this same knowledge. This manifestation is not insight into a particular subject and is not revelation knowledge in the context that we believers usually use it. It is a manifestation triggered by the Holy Ghost. It is the awareness of facts concerning a matter brought to the mind of a person by the Holy Ghost. It is not knowledge from memory, thought or imagination even though the knowledge needs to enter the thoughts of a person in order for them to be able to relate and act on the knowledge.

We cannot *learn* the word of knowledge, the same way you cannot *teach* a believer to speak in tongues. We can teach about it, but it is not like learning a new natural language where you can buy books on the words and how to pronounce the words. We can only be taught about the word of knowledge and its operations. Just like in the case of tongues, a gift the believer receives when the Holy Ghost comes upon them (*Acts 1:8, 2:4*), the word of knowledge is a gift that manifests as the Spirit wills.

> ⁸ **BUT YE SHALL RECEIVE POWER, AFTER THAT THE HOLY GHOST IS COME UPON YOU:** *and ye shall be witnesses unto me both in Jerusalem, and in all Judaea, and in Samaria, and unto the uttermost part of the earth.*
>
> *Acts 1:8*
>
> ² *And suddenly there came a sound from heaven as of a rushing mighty wind, and it filled all the house where they were sitting.*
> ³ *And there appeared unto them cloven tongues like as of fire, and it sat upon each of them.*
> ⁴ **AND THEY WERE ALL FILLED WITH THE HOLY GHOST, AND BEGAN TO SPEAK WITH OTHER TONGUES, AS THE SPIRIT GAVE THEM UTTERANCE.**
>
> *Acts 2:2-4*

The word of knowledge manifests as the Spirit wills irrespective of the frequency of its operation in the believer. Some believers walk in a deeper level of ability than others in the operation of this gift and may sometimes seem like it is always on. There is no evidence in scripture to prove that the believer can manifest this gift or any of the other gifts of the Spirit at will.

> *¹¹ But all these worketh that one and the selfsame Spirit, DIVIDING TO EVERY MAN SEVERALLY AS HE WILL.*
>
> 1 Corinthians 12:11

This "*word of knowledge*" manifests as the Spirit wills. It is not something the speaker turns on and off at will. If this gift was based on the will of man or the actions of the mind, then we should be able walk around and supernaturally know something about everything every time, but this is not the case. Jesus, who walked in the ultimate measure (*John 4:34*) of anointing did not manifest this gift always, neither did any of the apostles.

The gift usually manifests to reveal something in the present or past. Let us look at some examples of the word of knowledge in operation in the ministry of Jesus.

> *¹ And he entered into a ship, and passed over, and came into his own city.*
> *² And, behold, they brought to him a man sick of the palsy, lying on a bed: and Jesus seeing their faith said unto the sick of the palsy; Son, be of good cheer; thy sins be forgiven thee.*
> *³ And, behold, CERTAIN OF THE SCRIBES SAID WITHIN THEMSELVES, This man blasphemeth.*
> *⁴ AND JESUS KNOWING THEIR THOUGHTS SAID, Wherefore think ye evil in your hearts?*
>
> Matthew 9:1-4

The scribes in this incident *said within themselves*. They had not spoken out their thoughts. They only said it within themselves, but Jesus knew their thoughts. How did He know their thoughts? By the Holy Spirit, through the gift of word of knowledge.

Someone might argue that Jesus must have heard the discussions they were having about the words He had spoken and therefore did not require the *word of knowledge* but look at the fourth verse of *Matthew 9*. It says *Jesus knew their thoughts* and asked *why think ye evil in your hearts?* Hold on! Where were they thinking evil? *"In their hearts"* Now, I am not aware of people who naturally know the thoughts of others. The only way thoughts are known is when they are expressed in words, writing or some other means of communication.

So what Jesus knew was in their thoughts and their hearts before the thoughts could be crystallised into a naturally understandable form . How then did Jesus know what they were thinking? *The word of knowledge.*

Looking at Luke's account of the same story, we have a clearer indication of how Jesus got to know the thought in the hearts of the scribes.

> [22] *But when Jesus* **PERCEIVED** *their thoughts, he answering said unto them, What reason ye in your hearts?*
>
> Luke 5:22

In this scripture, Jesus PERCEIVED their thoughts. The *greek* word used here is *"epiginosko"* which implies knowledge gained through supernatural revelation. It is not knowledge acquired through natural means.

Another example of the manifestation of this gift is seen in the story of the woman at the well in Samaria.

> [7] *There cometh a woman of Samaria to draw water: Jesus saith unto her, Give me to drink.*
> [8] *(For his disciples were gone away unto the city to buy meat.)*
> [9] *Then saith the woman of Samaria unto him, How is it that thou, being a Jew, askest drink of me, which am a woman of Samaria? for the Jews have no dealings with the Samaritans.*
> [10] *Jesus answered and said unto her, If thou knewest the gift of God, and who it is that saith to thee, Give me to drink; thou wouldest have asked of him, and he would have given thee living water.*

Knowledge and the gift of word of Knowledge

¹¹ The woman saith unto him, Sir, thou hast nothing to draw with, and the well is deep: from whence then hast thou that living water?
¹² Art thou greater than our father Jacob, which gave us the well, and drank thereof himself, and his children, and his cattle?
¹³ Jesus answered and said unto her, Whosoever drinketh of this water shall thirst again:
¹⁴ But whosoever drinketh of the water that I shall give him shall never thirst; but the water that I shall give him shall be in him a well of water springing up into everlasting life.
¹⁵ The woman saith unto him, Sir, give me this water, that I thirst not, neither come hither to draw.
¹⁶ Jesus saith unto her, Go, call thy husband, and come hither.
¹⁷ THE WOMAN ANSWERED AND SAID, I HAVE NO HUSBAND. JESUS SAID UNTO HER, THOU HAST WELL SAID, I HAVE NO HUSBAND: 18 FOR THOU HAST HAD FIVE HUSBANDS; AND HE WHOM THOU NOW HAST IS NOT THY HUSBAND: IN THAT SAIDST THOU TRULY.
¹⁹ The woman saith unto him, Sir, I perceive that thou art a prophet.

John 4:7-19

How did Jesus know this woman had had five husbands even though we have no record of them having met prior to this occasion? By the Holy Spirit through the manifestation of the gift of *word of knowledge*.

This woman's response also provides some insight into what actually took place.

¹⁹ *The woman saith unto him,* SIR, I PERCEIVE THAT THOU ART A PROPHET.

John 4:19

She immediately associated what Jesus had done to what she must have known {*knowledge gained through natural means*} about the working of the Holy Spirit in prophets. Prophets have supernatural revelation of the mind of God on circumstances of life. As prophets are vessels used by God for bringing revelation to the world, it is more likely to have gifts of the Holy Spirit that reveal things manifesting more often in them than in other people who do not stand

Page | 21

in this office. This, of course, does not mean everyone who the word of knowledge manifests through is a prophet.

Notice that this woman also PERCEIVED something. So was this supernatural revelation as well? No. In this case, the *greek* word translated *"perceive"* is *"theoreo"* which means *to look closely upon or behold as a spectator watching an event.* This indicates there must have been something about Jesus that gave this woman the impression he was a prophet. There was something discernable from the events unfolding that gave Jesus away.

Let us look at this example from Elisha the prophet that lived in the Old Testament.

> [20] *But Gehazi, the servant of Elisha the man of God, said, Behold, my master hath spared Naaman this Syrian, in not receiving at his hands that which he brought: but, as the LORD liveth, I will run after him, and take somewhat of him.*
> [21] *So Gehazi followed after Naaman. And when Naaman saw him running after him, he lighted down from the chariot to meet him, and said, Is all well?*
> [22] *And he said, All is well. My master hath sent me, saying, Behold, even now there be come to me from mount Ephraim two young men of the sons of the prophets: give them, I pray thee, a talent of silver, and two changes of garments.*
> [23] *And Naaman said, Be content, take two talents. And he urged him, and bound two talents of silver in two bags, with two changes of garments, and laid them upon two of his servants; and they bare them before him.*
> [24] *And when he came to the tower, he took them from their hand, and bestowed them in the house: and he let the men go, and they departed.*
> [25] *But he went in, and stood before his master. And Elisha said unto him, Whence comest thou, Gehazi? And he said, Thy servant went no whither.*
> [26] *AND HE SAID UNTO HIM, WENT NOT MINE HEART WITH THEE, when the man turned again from his chariot to meet thee? Is it a time to receive money, and to receive garments, and oliveyards, and*

vineyards, and sheep, and oxen, and menservants, and maidservants?

2 Kings 5:20-26

Elisha did not leave where he was but when Gehazi came back he could describe in such detail what had happened to Gehazi on the trip he had just been on. Notice Elisha's comment in *verse 26*. How does you heart travel with someone? What Elisha was describing here is not a physical situation. It appears Elisha also saw something in the process. The word of knowledge can manifest in different ways and the believer has not control over this. That is why it is by faith.

I remember a meeting I was holding in Nigeria a number of years back. Just after the ministration of the Word of God, the Spirit of the Lord was present and suddenly I started to describe an incident that had happened between a student and a lecturer and how God was going to change a situation in favour of this particular student. I did not see anything in this case, it just came as if someone had told me a story and I narrated what I had heard. The important thing about this is that, God always uses these manifestations to bless His people.

God is the fountain of knowledge, and all things are open and naked before His eyes. (*Hebrews 4:13*). When the gift of *word of knowledge* manifests, God brings us into a fraction of His knowledge concerning a particular issue. It is as if the lid is taken off something and we are allowed to take a peek.

As believers, we need both forms of knowledge and we can ask God who gives liberally for such knowledge.

Chapter Key Points

Without God, there is no knowledge. He is the author of knowledge and the fountain of inspiration

Any branch cut from a tree always falls downward. It never goes up. In like manner, anyone cut-off from God always goes down and falls short of glory

We cannot *learn* the word of knowledge, the same way you cannot *teach* a believer to speak in tongues

This gift manifests as the Spirit wills. It is not something the speaker turns on and off at will

3

Qualifying for Knowledge

As we look deeper into the knowledge that comes from God, someone might wonder if there are any prerequisites for this kind of knowledge. You may even wonder if it is only for a select few with priviledged backgrounds. The more you look at the Word of God in the Bible, the more you see that the best of God is available to *ALL* who meet His condition of faith.

We all, irrespective of background, nationality, race or ethnicity have the capacity to believe what we hear. This is all faith is, believing in the written and revealed Word of God and acting like it is true. The fundamental criteria for qualifying for this knowledge is believing what God has said about it. All Abraham, the father of faith did, was to believe that what God had said, God was able to perform. Abraham held on, even when the physical senses told a contradicting story. It takes faith to receive anything from God and the knowledge we are talking about is no different.

Too many times, we miss out on the best of God because we fail to receive. The lack of manifestation, in many situations is not with God giving, it is with us receiving. It is always said that Abraham believed God for the birth of Isaac and this is true but it was not only Abraham's faith in operation. Sarah also had to walk in faith.

> *11 Through faith also Sara herself received strength to conceive seed, and was delivered of a child when she was past age, because she judged him faithful who had promised.*
>
> *Hebrews 11:11*

What! Sarah who laughed exercised faith? As Sarah judged him faithful, we also need to judge Him faithful. We need to receive strength through faith to conceive the seed of knowledge. Faith is the stepping stone for those disqualified and looked down upon by society. Through faith, we have access to the same resources as the most privileged. For blessings that last, receiving always comes before manifestation. Without a promise from above, there is no guarantee of a manifestation.

> *24 Therefore I say unto you, What things soever ye desire, when ye pray, believe that ye receive them, and ye shall have them.*
>
> *Mark 11:24*

Jesus says we should believe we receive and we shall have. Why is it important for us to *believe we receive*? A lot of the qualifications required by Nebu-chad-nez'-zar can only be achieved by believing in faith. Not many are born royals, not many can stay without blemish, not many possess the ability to stand before kings without having an inferiority complex. Through faith in the completed work of Jesus, we are able to claim all the requirements for this knowledge.

It is interesting that Nebu-chad-nez'-zar did not search for these children with knowledge among his own people, he went into the midst of *prisoners of war* to seek children *cunning in knowledge*. Did he not have more qualified people already in his kingdom that could have met his requirement? After all, they had just demonstrated superior military might by conquering the children of Israel. (*Daniel 1:1-2*).

This action of Nebu-chad-nez'-zar is very symbolic. Even if we find ourselves as prisoners in the prison of life or a minority in a foreign land, there is hope. Joseph was a minority and a prisoner in a foreign land, yet he ascended to a position of eminence. Remember, only believe you receive and it will become a reality. The image you build in your mind by the word of God is the possible future you can enjoy if you hold on till the end. Every visionless mind produces an impactless future. A mind void of revelation is a mind empty of expectation. This expectation is what produces hope and hope is what faith gives substance to. Without hope there is nothing for faith to give substance to (*Hebrews 11:1*).

It does not matter what position, location, ethnicity or race you find yourself, you can be part of the majority yet irrelevant. You may also be regarded as an ethnic minority, yet highly favoured of God and have the destiny of the land in your hands. The Bible declares *"that which the builders have rejected is become the chief corner stone"* If you have been despised, rejected, abused by men or born into a seemingly deprived environment, rejoice, for the God of favour has highly favoured you and the time for elevation is now here. As these boys were selected by the king, you have also been selected by the King of kings.

Let us look at the qualification criteria the king put forward for the selection of these Hebrew boys and see how our inheritance in Christ qualifies us for the same. For while we were yet sinners, Christ died for us and qualified us. This qualification in Christ is not based on works but by the grace of God, that we all may have a chance at this wonderful opportunity. Glory to God!

King Nebu-chad-nez'-zar was very specific about what he wanted in these Hebrew boys. Let us read his request again.

> ³ And the king spake unto Ashpenaz the master of his eunuchs, that he should bring certain of the children of Israel, and of the king's seed, and of the princes;
> ⁴ Children in whom was no blemish, but well favoured, and skilful in all wisdom, and cunning in knowledge, and understanding science, and such as had ability in them to stand in the king's palace, and whom they might teach the learning and the tongue of the Chaldeans.
>
> Daniel 1:3-4

Children of Israel, of kings seed and of princes

I wondered what the significance of picking the children from this presumably limited pool relative to all the children taken captive was and I realised that picking from this pool meant that certain foundational thoughts, concepts and behavioural patterns would already have been acquired by this children, simply because of their birth roots. The possibilities available to a living thing is usually determined by the *roots or seed* from which the thing emerges. So for example, I do not think there is much you can do to the egg of a lizard to make it hatch into a lion. The very fact that the egg came from a lizard has defined the possibilities that can exist for whatever comes out of the egg.

In order words, belonging to the tribe of royalty, that is, the tribe of Israel should deliver wisdom, etiquette and potential for growth and all the other things that Nebu-chad-nez'-zar required. With the kind of lineage these children belonged to, they probably could have progressed into being eligible for election as kings, had they not been taken into captivity.

Interestingly, the heritage of the Believer that has accepted Jesus Christ as Lord and Saviour places us in a position similar to these children, prior to them being taken into captivity. The journey starts with being born-again. When a sinner becomes born-again, the seed of the King of kings is implanted in them, making them take on characteristics similar to the seed. If no limitation exists in God, how can what comes out of him be limited? The limitation man experiences today is not one set by God, it is one set by the entrance of sin, granted by Adam. Once this sin is eradicated, the mentality of possibility returns. Let us see some scriptures that make this possible.

[23] *Being born again, not of corruptible seed, but of incorruptible, by the word of God, which liveth and abideth for ever.*

1 Peter 1:23

If we are born again by a seed and we know that seed is designed to reproduce after its kind, surely the seed should grow in us and cause us to take on characteristics similar to the nature of the seed by which we were born-again.

[12] *And the earth brought forth grass, AND HERB YIELDING SEED AFTER HIS KIND, and THE TREE YIELDING FRUIT, WHOSE SEED WAS IN ITSELF, AFTER HIS KIND: and God saw that it was good.*

Genesis 1:12

An orange tree will always produce oranges and an apple tree will always produce apples. There is nothing you can do to a dog to make it give birth to an elephant nor to an giraffe to make it give birth to a lion. Seed always reproduces after its kind.

If we are born of incorruptible seed, then we must be like the seed that gave birth to us.

> ³ Blessed be the God and Father of our Lord Jesus Christ, **WHICH ACCORDING TO HIS ABUNDANT MERCY HATH BEGOTTEN US AGAIN** unto a lively hope by the resurrection of Jesus Christ from the dead,
> ⁴ **TO AN INHERITANCE INCORRUPTIBLE, AND UNDEFILED**, and that fadeth not away, reserved in heaven for you,
>
> 1 Peter 1:3-4

What did this *"begetting"* turn us into?

> ⁹ But ye are a chosen generation, a royal priesthood, an holy nation, a peculiar people; that ye should shew forth the praises of him who hath called you out of darkness into his marvellous light;
> ¹⁰ Which in time past were not a people, but are now the people of God: which had not obtained mercy, but now have obtained mercy.
>
> 1 Peter 2:9-10

Hallelujah! In times past, we were not a people, but now the people of God, a chosen generation and royalty.

> ¹⁰ And hast made us unto our God kings and priests: and we shall reign on the earth.
>
> Revelation 5:10

Having been given this power or authority to become sons of God (*John 1: 12*), we qualify for this criteria. Glory be to God. Remember, the seed of God makes you more than spiritual, it makes you a spirit.

> ²⁴ God is a Spirit: and they that worship him must worship him in spirit and in truth.
>
> John 4:24

> ⁵ Jesus answered, Verily, verily, I say unto thee, Except a man be born of water and of the Spirit, he cannot enter into the kingdom of God.

> *⁶ That which is born of the flesh is flesh; and that which is born of the Spirit is spirit.*
>
> *John 3:5-6*

God is a Spirit, therefore when He gives birth, He gives birth to a spirit. Being spiritual is the process of acting like you are a spiritual personality manifesting characteristics of the seed that gave birth to you.

No Blemish

The Hebrew word used for *blemish* in the scriptures here refers to physical or moral stains or spots. It includes scars in parts of the body that are not visible to others while not excluding physical handicap.

> *⁴ CHILDREN IN WHOM WAS NO BLEMISH, but well favoured, and skilful in all wisdom, and cunning in knowledge, and understanding science, and such as had ability in them to stand in the king's palace, and whom they might teach the learning and the tongue of the Chaldeans.*
>
> *Daniel 1:3-4*

In these days we live in, any selection based on physical *"blemishes"* could be regarded as discriminatory, attracting the wrath of the laws of the land. These physical handicaps are not as important as the moral or spiritual ones which deal with the hidden wounds and scars of the heart. These hidden blemishes show themselves in the words that proceed from the mouth of scarred hearts and are destiny destroyers. Business deals are known to have been lost simply because people spoke out of anger or hurt. Relationships have been destroyed because of these same hidden scars and marriages have also been destroyed because of hidden wounds.

A lot of violent crime today is being linked to wounds that were inflicted on hearts while young but have taken years to manifest. When these manifestations takes place, it is often at unpredictable times and places.

However, the word of God makes us know that the blood of Jesus can cleanse these internal wounds.

> ⁷ But if we walk in the light, as he is in the light, we have fellowship one with another, and **THE BLOOD OF JESUS CHRIST HIS SON CLEANSETH US FROM ALL SIN.**
> ⁸ If we say that we have no sin, we deceive ourselves, and the truth is not in us.
> ⁹ If we confess our sins, he is faithful and just to forgive us our sins, and to cleanse us from all unrighteousness.
>
> 1 John 1:7-9

Sin is like a stain on the heart of man. It blocks the part of the heart from which the issues of life flow but the blood of Jesus is more powerful than ALL sin. It is this blood of Jesus that makes us without blemish and cleanses us from all these scars.

> ¹⁴ In whom we have redemption through his blood, even the forgiveness of sins:
>
> Colossians 1:14

God also declares that *"their sins will I remember no more"*. We qualify for this criteria by the wonderful act of God the Father through Jesus on the cross of calvary.

Well Favoured

Favour is an aura you carry that make others respond in a respectable manner towards you and the things that concern you. Favour is the inward presence that exudes from you as a well pleasing aroma in the sight of others.

This aroma will make others want to do anything in their power to maintain your graceful state. Sometimes, this is not based on anything you have done but just on a series of coincidental occurrences showing steps that are ordered by God.

> *⁴ Children in whom was no blemish, **BUT WELL FAVOURED**, and skilful in all wisdom, and cunning in knowledge, and understanding science, and such as had ability in them to stand in the king's palace, and whom they might teach the learning and the tongue of the Chaldeans.*
>
> *Daniel 1:3-4*

King Nebu-chad-nez'-zar was looking for well favoured children who were not just favoured but had the proofs or evidence of the favour in the eyes of others. They must have been referred to as favoured by others, showing the approval of God. (*Acts 2:22*). Favour is not just an inward virtue. It provokes physical manifestations that are recognisable by others. Favour cannot be hidden. If favour is present, unusual manifestations are usually not far away.

The Psalmist describes this favour in Psalm 16:6

> *⁶ The lines are fallen unto me in pleasant places; yea, I have a goodly heritage.*
>
> *Psalm 16:6*

Again in another place the Psalmist says:

> *⁶ Surely goodness and mercy shall follow me all the days of my life: and I will dwell in the house of the LORD for ever.*
>
> *Psalm 23:6*

The prophet Isaiah also describes this favour is such graphic form.

> ¹ Arise, shine; for thy light is come, and the glory of the LORD is risen upon thee.
> ² For, behold, the darkness shall cover the earth, and gross darkness the people: but the LORD shall arise upon thee, and his glory shall be seen upon thee.
> ³ And the Gentiles shall come to thy light, and kings to the brightness of thy rising.
> ⁴ Lift up thine eyes round about, and see: all they gather themselves together, they come to thee: thy sons shall come from far, and thy daughters shall be nursed at thy side.
> ⁵ Then thou shalt see, and flow together, and thine heart shall fear, and be enlarged; because the abundance of the sea shall be converted unto thee, the forces of the Gentiles shall come unto thee.
> ⁶ The multitude of camels shall cover thee, the dromedaries of Midian and Ephah; all they from Sheba shall come: they shall bring gold and incense; and they shall shew forth the praises of the LORD.
> ⁷ All the flocks of Kedar shall be gathered together unto thee, the rams of Nebaioth shall minister unto thee: they shall come up with acceptance on mine altar, and I will glorify the house of my glory.
>
> Isaiah 60:1-7

These riches of the Gentiles flow to the people of God because the glory of the Lord is risen upon them and they are highly favoured. To be well favoured is for the forces of the earth to respond to you. It is when people you do not know are inclined to give resources to you. Do you remember the donkey Jesus used for the triumphant entry and the upper room that was made ready for him? This favourable disposition toward you is not something you only get from people that love you. When your ways please the Lord, *even your enemies* will be at peace with you (*Proverbs 16:7*).

> ³⁶ And the LORD gave the people favour in the sight of the Egyptians, so that they lent unto them such things as they required. And they spoiled the Egyptians.
>
> Exodus 12:36

Qualifying for the Knowledge

It was favour that gave the Hebrew boys the ten days they needed to prove that they did not need the kings portion of food. If God had not given them favour, they may have missed this opportunity to prove their God was alive.

> [9] Now God had brought Daniel into favour and tender love with the prince of the eunuchs.
> [10] And the prince of the eunuchs said unto Daniel, I fear my lord the king, who hath appointed your meat and your drink: for why should he see your faces worse liking than the children which are of your sort? then shall ye make me endanger my head to the king.
> [11] Then said Daniel to Melzar, whom the prince of the eunuchs had set over Daniel, Hananiah, Mishael, and Azariah,
> [12] Prove thy servants, I beseech thee, ten days; and let them give us pulse to eat, and water to drink.
> [13] Then let our countenances be looked upon before thee, and the countenance of the children that eat of the portion of the king's meat: and as thou seest, deal with thy servants.
> [14] So he consented to them in this matter, and proved them ten days.
>
> Daniel 1:9-14

To fully understand the power of favour, we need to look at the story of the children of Israel while they were in Egypt. In the days of Joseph, they lived in the land of Goshen, in plenty and flourishing though the rest of the land was in a famine but what happened after Joseph died to change the destiny of a people for four hundred years? Another king arose that did not know Joseph or any of the works of Joseph and the fountain of favour dried up.

> [7] And the children of Israel were fruitful, and increased abundantly, and multiplied, and waxed exceeding mighty; and the land was filled with them.
> [8] NOW THERE AROSE UP A NEW KING OVER EGYPT, WHICH KNEW NOT JOSEPH.
> [9] And he said unto his people, Behold, the people of the children of Israel are more and mightier than we:
> [10] Come on, let us deal wisely with them; lest they multiply, and it

> *come to pass, that, when there falleth out any war, they join also unto our enemies, and fight against us, and so get them up out of the land.*
> *¹¹ Therefore they did set over them taskmasters to afflict them with their burdens. And they built for Pharaoh treasure cities, Pithom and Raamses.*
> *¹² But the more they afflicted them, the more they multiplied and grew. And they were grieved because of the children of Israel.*
> *¹³ And the Egyptians made the children of Israel to serve with rigour:*
> *¹⁴ AND THEY MADE THEIR LIVES BITTER WITH HARD BONDAGE, IN MORTER, AND IN BRICK, AND IN ALL MANNER OF SERVICE IN THE FIELD: ALL THEIR SERVICE, WHEREIN THEY MADE THEM SERVE, WAS WITH RIGOUR.*
>
> Exodus 1:7-14

When the favour of God is present with you, the affairs of your life will work without tears. The works of your hands will not require unnecessary rigour like the children of Israel.

As a messenger of God to the church, I declare in the name of Jesus, that all bitterness and bondage that may have tormented you, seize now. I command a cloud of favour to break forth with rain over you from this day forward. Return with joy and gladness, let the light of His glory break forth over you in Jesus name. From today, people you do not know will favour you. You increase sweatlessly.

Favour is as dew on the grass (*Psalm 23:2*) and as a cloud of rain on fallow ground. The first apostles enjoyed this same favour which led to their increase. Favour always brings increase by multiplication.

> *⁴⁷ Praising God, and having favour with all the people. And the Lord added to the church daily such as should be saved.*
>
> Acts 2:47

Favour can be from men or from God but the favour of the Lord is always more important than the favour of men and if the Lord has not favoured you, be rest assured, men will not have it in them to favour you.

> [26] Many seek the ruler's favour; but every man's judgment cometh from the LORD.
>
> Proverbs 29:26
>
> [4] So shalt thou find favour and good understanding in the sight of God and man.
>
> Proverbs 3:4

Favour should not be taken lightly. It could be the difference between toiling without result and productivity without tears. It was through favour that Mary the mother of Jesus was selected (*Luke 1:30*) to be the channel through which the word of God became flesh (*John 1:14*). More often than not in our prayers, even after we have received what we have believed for, we need favour to obtain the physical manifestation of our prayers.

There are different measures of favour, making favour something we grow in. In *Luke 2:52*, we see that Jesus *increased* in favour with God and man. So favour is a virtue that can be increased. It was God who brought Daniel into favour with the prince of the eunuchs (*Daniel 1:9*). Favour with God will always bring you into favour with man.

Skilful in Wisdom

To be wise is a great asset, to be skilful in the use of wisdom is an even greater asset. Nebu-chad-nez'-zar wanted children skilful in ALL wisdom. What does this mean? ALL indicates that the wisdom referred to here could be broken down into components. Nebu-chad-nez'-zar wanted children who possessed all the components.

> ⁴ *Children in whom was no blemish, but well favoured, and* SKILFUL IN ALL WISDOM, *and cunning in knowledge, and understanding science, and such as had ability in them to stand in the king's palace, and whom they might teach the learning and the tongue of the Chaldeans.*
>
> Daniel 1:3-4

Wisdom here means the power or ability to demonstrate discernment and discretion in mind, words and actions coupled with an ability to teach it to others. It is possible to be wise in mind and words but not in actions. This is the situation James the apostle referred to when he wrote about people who were hearers of the word of God but not doers (*James 1:22*). You can know all the right words and all the principles available to arouse action but unless you act, what you know is useless.

Acting in wisdom is a conscious activity. It is very easy to let the *"actions"* part of wisdom slip particularly if you are involved in teaching it. How can you explain Solomon marrying one thousand wives and three hundred concubines, yet being one of the wisest men to have lived? With all his wisdom he should have known that the heart of a man is not designed to express affectionate love to more than one woman at the same time. You will either love one and hate the other or love none. If you love someone with all your heart, there is no part of it left with which you can love another. The true test of love is the readiness of the lover to give all and all includes life. Can you imagine if Jesus had to make choices on who to give His life for? His bride the Church or other brides.

Remember Nebu-chad-nez'-zar wanted children skilful in the use of wisdom. The word *skilful* used here literally means to execute wise instructions like an expert. Jesus gave us a promise that ensures such wisdom is available to us.

> ¹⁴ Settle it therefore in your hearts, not to meditate before what ye shall answer:
> ¹⁵ For I will give you a mouth and wisdom, which all your adversaries shall not be able to gainsay nor resist.
>
> Luke 21:14-15

This wisdom silences the adversaries. Look at the example of Jesus, when the Pharisees were gathered together.

> ⁴¹ While the Pharisees were gathered together, Jesus asked them,
> ⁴² Saying, What think ye of Christ? whose son is he? They say unto him, The son of David.
> ⁴³ He saith unto them, How then doth David in spirit call him Lord, saying,
> ⁴⁴ The LORD said unto my Lord, Sit thou on my right hand, till I make thine enemies thy footstool?
> ⁴⁵ If David then call him Lord, how is he his son?
> ⁴⁶ AND NO MAN WAS ABLE TO ANSWER HIM A WORD, NEITHER DURST ANY MAN FROM THAT DAY FORTH ASK HIM ANY MORE QUESTIONS.
>
> Matthew 22:41-46

Another example of Jesus walking in this dimension of wisdom is seen in *Luke 20*.

> ¹ And it came to pass, that on one of those days, as he taught the people in the temple, and preached the gospel, the chief priests and the scribes came upon him with the elders,
> ² And spake unto him, saying, Tell us, by what authority doest thou these things? or who is he that gave thee this authority?
> ³ And he answered and said unto them, I will also ask you one thing; and answer me:
> ⁴ The baptism of John, was it from heaven, or of men?
> ⁵ And they reasoned with themselves, saying, If we shall say, From heaven; he will say, Why then believed ye him not?
> ⁶ But and if we say, Of men; all the people will stone us: for they be persuaded that John was a prophet.
> ⁷ And they answered, that they could not tell whence it was.

> *⁸ And Jesus said unto them, Neither tell I you by what authority I do these things.*
>
> *Luke 20:1-8*

Because the Holy Spirit is in us, the study and practice of the Word of God brings to us a superior dimension of wisdom compared to anything available to the world. I am not just referring to *"spiritual"* understanding and wisdom here, I am referring to spiritual wisdom with tangible results that forcefully establish the kingdom of our God on the earth. It is about the spiritual light that shines in the believer and eradicates poverty.

> *⁹⁹ I have more understanding than all my teachers: for thy testimonies are my meditation.*
> *¹⁰⁰ I understand more than the ancients, because I keep thy precepts.*
>
> *Psalm 119:99-100*

The Lord is able to give such wisdom to all who believe, say not it is too high, it pleases Him to lavish such wisdom on His children. His wisdom is available to all who ask. Ask that you may receive, Ask that you may excel, Ask that you may rise above the wisdom of the world. His wisdom is pure, His wisdom is from the Spirit. His wisdom is for his children.

Solomon was another person who walked in this unusual wisdom.

> *¹⁶ Then came there two women, that were harlots, unto the king, and stood before him.*
> *¹⁷ And the one woman said, O my lord, I and this woman dwell in one house; and I was delivered of a child with her in the house.*
> *¹⁸ And it came to pass the third day after that I was delivered, that this woman was delivered also: and we were together; there was no stranger with us in the house, save we two in the house.*
> *¹⁹ And this woman's child died in the night; because she overlaid it.*
> *²⁰ And she arose at midnight, and took my son from beside me, while*

thine handmaid slept, and laid it in her bosom, and laid her dead child in my bosom.
²¹ And when I rose in the morning to give my child suck, behold, it was dead: but when I had considered it in the morning, behold, it was not my son, which I did bear.
²² And the other woman said, Nay; but the living is my son, and the dead is thy son. And this said, No; but the dead is thy son, and the living is my son. Thus they spake before the king.
²³ Then said the king, The one saith, This is my son that liveth, and thy son is the dead: and the other saith, Nay; but thy son is the dead, and my son is the living.
²⁴ And the king said, Bring me a sword. And they brought a sword before the king.
²⁵ And the king said, Divide the living child in two, and give half to the one, and half to the other.
²⁶ Then spake the woman whose the living child was unto the king, for her bowels yearned upon her son, and she said, O my lord, give her the living child, and in no wise slay it. But the other said, Let it be neither mine nor thine, but divide it.
²⁷ Then the king answered and said, Give her the living child, and in no wise slay it: she is the mother thereof.
²⁸ And all Israel heard of the judgment which the king had judged; and they feared the king: for they saw that the wisdom of God was in him, to do judgment.

1 Kings 3:16-28

Solomon's wisdom was next to none in his time and his judgement in this case is testament to that. That national leaders came to hear Solomon's wisdom is confirmation that relying totally on God for wisdom does not mean living in obscurity. God's wisdom brings with it a brightness that can be seen from afar.

Cunning in Knowledge

This is a very specific requirement that implies the ability to draw conclusions or new ideas from existing information, without prior preparation. This refers to the wise utilisation of knowledge. It is the sort of knowledge required for inventions. It is the knowledge that makes people dissatisfied with the status quo. This is the ability that leads to creativity.

> *[4] Children in whom was no blemish, but well favoured, and skilful in all wisdom, and CUNNING IN KNOWLEDGE, and understanding science, and such as had ability in them to stand in the king's palace, and whom they might teach the learning and the tongue of the Chaldeans.*
>
> Daniel 1:3-4

Such cunning knowledge was demonstrated in the time of Uzziah.

> *[15] And he made in Jerusalem engines, INVENTED BY CUNNING MEN, to be on the towers and upon the bulwarks, to shoot arrows and great stones withal. And his name spread far abroad; for he was marvellously helped, till he was strong.*
>
> 2 Chronicles 26:8-15

Another example of this ability in seen when Moses was building the temple of the Lord, following the instruction of God.

> *[1] And the LORD spake unto Moses, saying,*
> *[2] See, I have called by name Bezaleel the son of Uri, the son of Hur, of the tribe of Judah:*
> *[3] AND I HAVE FILLED HIM WITH THE SPIRIT OF GOD, IN WISDOM, AND IN UNDERSTANDING, AND IN KNOWLEDGE, AND IN ALL MANNER OF WORKMANSHIP,*
> *4 TO DEVISE CUNNING WORKS, to work in gold, and in silver, and in brass,*
> *[5] And in cutting of stones, to set them, and in carving of timber, to work in all manner of workmanship.*
>
> Exodus 31:1-5

Bezaleel would not have been able to do the wood work

of the temple if God had not anointed or enabled him. Believers need to be aware that ministry gifts are not only the five-fold gifts mentioned in *Ephesians 4:11*. Everyone that takes part in doing anything for God requires an enabling ability from God. Notice that one of the gifts from God was the Spirit of Knowledge *(Isaiah 11:1-2)*. In the early days in the Church, even the serving of tables required men full of the Holy Ghost and wisdom *(Acts 6:1-3)*. These days the modern church seems to be oscillating between no training at all because we are desperate for hands to put to the plough and too formal training because we want to be professional while the key ingredients of good report, Holy Ghost and wisdom are treated as secondary.

King Solomon possessed this kind of knowledge.

> [29] **AND GOD GAVE SOLOMON WISDOM AND UNDERSTANDING EXCEEDING MUCH, AND LARGENESS OF HEART, EVEN AS THE SAND THAT IS ON THE SEA SHORE.**
> [30] *And Solomon's wisdom excelled the wisdom of all the children of the east country, and all the wisdom of Egypt.*
> [31] *For he was wiser than all men; than Ethan the Ezrahite, and Heman, and Chalcol, and Darda, the sons of Mahol: and his fame was in all nations round about.*
> [32] *And he spake three thousand proverbs: and his songs were a thousand and five.*
> [33] **AND HE SPAKE OF TREES, FROM THE CEDAR TREE THAT IS IN LEBANON EVEN UNTO THE HYSSOP THAT SPRINGETH OUT OF THE WALL: HE SPAKE ALSO OF BEASTS, AND OF FOWL, AND OF CREEPING THINGS, AND OF FISHES.**
> [34] *And there came of all people to hear the wisdom of Solomon, from all kings of the earth, which had heard of his wisdom.*
>
> 1 Kings 4:29-34

But how did Solomon get all this wisdom, knowledge and understanding considering he referred to himself as a little child?

> [7] *And now, O LORD my God, thou hast made thy servant king instead*

of David my father: and I am but a little child: I know not how to go out or come in.

⁸ And thy servant is in the midst of thy people which thou hast chosen, a great people, that cannot be numbered nor counted for multitude.

⁹ Give therefore thy servant an understanding heart to judge thy people, that I may discern between good and bad: for who is able to judge this thy so great a people?

¹⁰ And the speech pleased the LORD, that Solomon had asked this thing.

¹¹ And God said unto him, Because thou hast asked this thing, and hast not asked for thyself long life; neither hast asked riches for thyself, nor hast asked the life of thine enemies; but hast asked for thyself understanding to discern judgment;

¹² Behold, I have done according to thy words: lo, I have given thee a wise and an understanding heart; so that there was none like thee before thee, neither after thee shall any arise like unto thee.

¹³ And I have also given thee that which thou hast not asked, both riches, and honour: so that there shall not be any among the kings like unto thee all thy days.

¹⁴ And if thou wilt walk in my ways, to keep my statutes and my commandments, as thy father David did walk, then I will lengthen thy days.

¹⁵ And Solomon awoke; and, behold, it was a dream. And he came to Jerusalem, and stood before the ark of the covenant of the LORD, and offered up burnt offerings, and offered peace offerings, and made a feast to all his servants.

1 Kings 3:7-15

This kind of knowledge and largeness of heart demonstrated by Solomon is available to the believer today. The same God who was rich to Solomon even fills us with an abundance of revelation because we are established on a better promise. As Solomon asked God and received such wisdom and largeness of heart, God has made provision for us under the new Covenant to walk in newness of life in where know all things. There is a breath in us and inspiration that wells up as supernatural knowledge.

[20] *But ye have an unction from the Holy One, and ye know all things.*

1 John 2:20

Once we get born-again we are given the measure of faith (*Romans 12:3*) required to be able to take advantage of this blessing from God.

Understanding science

What has science got to do with standing in the presence of the King and what exactly is Science? Science is the organised and systematic study of facts through experimentation for the determination of a predictable set of results. These results lead to principles that govern the operation of the resources of the earth.

You may ask what has Christianity got to do with science, considering a lot of people tend to disregard Christianity because it cannot be scientifically proven. If God is the One who existed before the beginning of time, which He is, God must predate science as man knows it. God also demonstrates this kind of experimentation in the accounts of Himself we have in the Bible. He was the first scientist that ever existed. Let us see what He demonstrated in the book of Genesis.

> [1] *In the beginning God created the heaven and the earth.*
> [2] *And the earth was without form, and void; and darkness was upon the face of the deep. And the Spirit of God moved upon the face of the waters.*
> [3] *And God said, Let there be light: and there was light.*
> [4] **AND GOD SAW THE LIGHT, THAT IT WAS GOOD:** *and God divided the light from the darkness.*
> [5] *And God called the light Day, and the darkness he called Night. And the evening and the morning were the first day.*
> [6] *And God said, Let there be a firmament in the midst of the waters, and let it divide the waters from the waters.*

> ⁷ And God made the firmament, and divided the waters which were under the firmament from the waters which were above the firmament: and it was so.
> ⁸ And God called the firmament Heaven. And the evening and the morning were the second day.
> ⁹ And God said, Let the waters under the heaven be gathered together unto one place, and let the dry land appear: and it was so.
> ¹⁰ And God called the dry land Earth; and the gathering together of the waters called he Seas: **AND GOD SAW THAT IT WAS GOOD.**
> ¹¹ And God said, Let the earth bring forth grass, the herb yielding seed, and the fruit tree yielding fruit after his kind, whose seed is in itself, upon the earth: and it was so.
> ¹² And the earth brought forth grass, and herb yielding seed after his kind, and the tree yielding fruit, whose seed was in itself, after his kind: **AND GOD SAW THAT IT WAS GOOD.**
> ¹³ And the evening and the morning were the third day.
> ¹⁴ And God said, Let there be lights in the firmament of the heaven to divide the day from the night; and let them be for signs, and for seasons, and for days, and years:
> ¹⁵ And let them be for lights in the firmament of the heaven to give light upon the earth: and it was so.
>
> Genesis 1:1-15

In the story of creation, see the number of times *"God saw that it was good."* At every stage, He stopped to observe the facts, then continued to build. It almost gives the impression that if for any reason, He did not like what He saw, He would have destroyed it and started again. But can anything not good come out of God?

This same principle is described by prophet Isaiah:

> ¹⁰ For precept must be upon precept, precept upon precept; line upon line, line upon line; here a little, and there a little:
>
> Isaiah 28:10

Many people are in too much of a hurry. We all want to get to day seven of creating our world without going through days two thru six, but notice God creates every thing that man will need before creating man himself. Quite often, God ensures everything to support the promise He has given us is in place before we see the physical manifestation. This is where patience shows up as the twin of faith. All practitioners of faith exercise patience.

For example, why did He have to wait seven days before creating man, why did the children of Israel have to wait four hundred years before being delivered from Egypt, why did Moses have to wait for the final sign of the death of the firstborn before delivering the children of Egypt. Was it not the same God that did the first miracle with the rod that did the last one? Everything God does is always time bound and tells a story about the person of God. It's all about Him. The story of life is in the journey. For all things there is an appointed time and an appointed season. Does a pregnant woman choose the time for her waters to break? This is why the prophet Zechariah wrote about asking for things while they may be found (*Zechariah 10:1*). For the waters of a pregnant woman to break in the second month of pregnancy is a bad sign. In other words, ask for things in the season of the thing (*Deuteronomy 11:14*). This principle of asking in season is what it means to pray the will of God concerning an issue. Find out the agenda of God and align yourself with it.

The story of creation as recorded in the book of Job also shows more details about this scientific approach to results.

> [4] *Where wast thou when I laid the foundations of the earth? declare, if thou hast understanding.*
> [5] *Who hath laid the measures thereof, if thou knowest? or who hath stretched the line upon it?*
> [6] *Whereupon are the foundations thereof fastened? or who laid the corner stone thereof;*
> [7] *When the morning stars sang together, and all the sons of God shouted for joy?*

> ⁸ Or who shut up the sea with doors, when it brake forth, as if it hthead issued out of the womb?
> ⁹ When I made the cloud the garment thereof, and thick darkness a swaddlingband for it,
> ¹⁰ And brake up for it my decreed place, and set bars and doors,
>
> Job 38:4-10

God first laid a foundation using lines and measures and then there was a corner stone. There were doors shutting up the seas. This shows the works of a very meticulous creator using exactly the right amount of resources and control where applicable. This sort of scientific understanding is also mentioned in the New Testament by Apostle Paul.

> ¹¹ When I was a child, I spake as a child, I understood as a child, I thought as a child: but when I became a man, I put away childish things.
>
> 1 Corinthians 13:11

There is the time for childish thinking, understanding and speech but there is also time for exhibiting traits of *"manhood"*. As more facts are understood, sometimes through experiments, people develop their thought processes and perceptions of life and as God they *"see it is good"*. Apostle Paul also talks about this developmental process.

> ¹¹ Of whom we have many things to say, and hard toak be uttered, seeing ye are dull of hearing.
> ¹² For when for the time ye ought to be teachers, ye have need that one teach you again which be the first principles of the oracles of God; and are become such as have need of milk, and not of strong meat.
> ¹³ For every one that useth milk is unskilful in the word of righteousness: for he is a babe.
> ¹⁴ But strong meat belongeth to them that are of full age, **EVEN THOSE WHO BY REASON OF USE HAVE THEIR SENSES EXERCISED TO DISCERN** both good and evil.
>
> Hebrews 5:11-14

To *"use"* in *verse 14* means *"having developed a habit from repeated use."* This repeated use is what leads to proficiency. As Christians, we need to develop proficiency in our area of interest through diligence and dedication.

This understanding of science is what also brings us into an understanding of times and seasons. This is the understanding required to launch products at the right time and into the right markets. It is the understanding that makes us succeed in markets where others have failed. This understanding of science gives the ability to understand patterns. Numerous times in the scriptures we are admonished to consider the ant and the eagle. What for? Patterns.

> *6 Go to the ant, thou sluggard; consider her ways, and be wise:*
>
> Proverbs 6:6

Looking at the eagle, we see an example of self induced change.

> *11 As an eagle stirreth up her nest, fluttereth over her young, spreadeth abroad her wings, taketh them, beareth them on her wings:*
> *12 So the LORD alone did lead him, and there was no strange god with him.*
>
> Deuteronomy 32:11-12

Understanding patterns is important because the same principle can be applied and built on for generating different results. For example, all air travel has to overcome the same force of gravity. All land travel must overcome the force of inertia for motion. Patterns can also be transferred from industry to industry causing a set of processes or management principles applied in one industry repeatable in another industry. The fact that we can transfer patterns from ants and birds to humans should be enough to convince you that to looking into other industries for solutions to problems in your industry may be a step in the right direction. This understanding of science is not given only to priviledged people. Every believer in the work of Jesus Christ has this understanding through the Holy Spirit. He is our guide that leads us and orders our steps.

> [13] Howbeit when he, the Spirit of truth, is come, he will guide you into all truth: for he shall not speak of himself; but whatsoever he shall hear, that shall he speak: and he will shew you things to come.
>
> John 16:13

The Holy Spirit is the One that opens our eyes to recognise these patterns so we need His help. We cannot rely on our own strength to do things.

Ability to stand in the kings presence

The presence of the king signifies the presence of a decision maker. In the Old Testament, one wrong word in the presence of a decision maker could not only end dreams but the life of a person. Look at the example of the Obadiah, a governor in the house of Ahab the king.

> [1] And it came to pass after many days, that the word of the LORD came to Elijah in the third year, saying, Go, shew thyself unto Ahab; and I will send rain upon the earth.
> [2] And Elijah went to shew himself unto Ahab. And there was a sore famine in Samaria.
> [3] And Ahab called Obadiah, which was the governor of his house. (Now Obadiah feared the LORD greatly:
> [4] For it was so, when Jezebel cut off the prophets of the LORD, that Obadiah took an hundred prophets, and hid them by fifty in a cave, and fed them with bread and water.)
> [5] And Ahab said unto Obadiah, Go into the land, unto all fountains of water, and unto all brooks: peradventure we may find grass to save the horses and mules alive, that we lose not all the beasts.
> [6] So they divided the land between them to pass throughout it: Ahab went one way by himself, and Obadiah went another way by himself.

⁷ And as Obadiah was in the way, behold, Elijah met him: and he knew him, and fell on his face, and said, Art thou that my lord Elijah?
⁸ And he answered him, I am: go, tell thy lord, Behold, Elijah is here.
⁹ And he said, What have I sinned, that thou wouldest deliver thy servant into the hand of Ahab, to slay me?
¹⁰ As the LORD thy God liveth, there is no nation or kingdom, whither my lord hath not sent to seek thee: and when they said, He is not there; he took an oath of the kingdom and nation, that they found thee not.
¹¹ And now thou sayest, Go, tell thy lord, Behold, Elijah is here.
¹² And it shall come to pass, as soon as I am gone from thee, that the Spirit of the LORD shall carry thee whither I know not; and so when I come and tell Ahab, and he cannot find thee, he shall slay me: but I thy servant fear the LORD from my youth.
¹³ Was it not told my lord what I did when Jezebel slew the prophets of the LORD, how I hid an hundred men of the LORD's prophets by fifty in a cave, and fed them with bread and water?
¹⁴ And now thou sayest, Go, tell thy lord, Behold, Elijah is here: and he shall slay me.
¹⁵ And Elijah said, As the LORD of hosts liveth, before whom I stand, I will surely shew myself unto him to day.
¹⁶ So Obadiah went to meet Ahab, and told him: and Ahab went to meet Elijah.

1 Kings 18:1-16

Obadiah understood the importance of making sure the words presented before the king were right. He therefore was not ready to take chances. Though protocol as practiced in royal palaces may not be as prevalent outside of royal circles, protocol is important and has a place in this present time. Disregard for a personal assistant may mean you do not get the favour of the decision maker. It may even mean you attract anger from him. Vashti, a queen in the days of Mordecai (*Esther 1-2:4*) experienced anger in this fashion because she did not respect the presence of the king.

¹³ Then the king said to the wise men, which knew the times, (for so was the king's manner toward all that knew law and judgment:
¹⁴ And the next unto him was Carshena, Shethar, Admatha, Tarshish, Meres, Marsena, and Memucan, the seven princes of Persia and

Media, which saw the king's face, and which sat the first in the kingdom;)

¹⁵ What shall we do unto the queen Vashti according to law, because she hath not performed the commandment of the king Ahasuerus by the chamberlains?

¹⁶ And Memucan answered before the king and the princes, Vashti the queen hath not done wrong to the king only, but also to all the princes, and to all the people that are in all the provinces of the king Ahasuerus.

¹⁷ For this deed of the queen shall come abroad unto all women, so that they shall despise their husbands in their eyes, when it shall be reported, The king Ahasuerus commanded Vashti the queen to be brought in before him, but she came not.

¹⁸ Likewise shall the ladies of Persia and Media say this day unto all the king's princes, which have heard of the deed of the queen. Thus shall there arise too much contempt and wrath.

¹⁹ If it please the king, let there go a royal commandment from him, and let it be written among the laws of the Persians and the Medes, that it be not altered, That Vashti come no more before king Ahasuerus; and let the king give her royal estate unto another that is better than she.

²⁰ And when the king's decree which he shall make shall be published throughout all his empire, (for it is great,) all the wives shall give to their husbands honour, both to great and small.

²¹ And the saying pleased the king and the princes; and the king did according to the word of Memucan:

²² For he sent letters into all the king's provinces, into every province according to the writing thereof, and to every people after their language, that every man should bear rule in his own house, and that it should be published according to the language of every people.

Esther 1:13-22

We need to be diligent in what we do to ensure we can stand in the kings presence. Diligence means chipping at the challenge a little at a time until a finished and desirable outcome is reached. It means not giving up too soon but enduring till the end.

²⁹ Seest thou a man diligent in his business? he shall stand before kings; he shall not stand before mean men.

Proverbs 22:29

Qualifying for the Knowledge

This ability to stand in the king's presence requires both inner confidence and outward appearance. Remember the story of Joseph, the premier of Egypt, just before going to meet Pharaoh.

> *¹⁴ Then Pharaoh sent and called Joseph, and they brought him hastily out of the dungeon: AND HE SHAVED HIMSELF, AND CHANGED HIS RAIMENT, and came in unto Pharaoh.*
>
> Genesis 41:14

The kings request was not too hasty for Joseph not to have time to shave and change his raiment. Esther who replaced Vashti in the story we just read spent twelve months preparing herself physically before going in to the kings presence.

> *¹² Now when every maid's turn was come to go in to king Ahasuerus, after that she had been twelve months, according to the manner of the women, (for so were the days of their purifications accomplished, to wit, six months with oil of myrrh, and six months with sweet odours, and with other things for the purifying of the women;)*
> *¹³ Then thus came every maiden unto the king; whatsoever she desired was given her to go with her out of the house of the women unto the king's house.*
> *¹⁴ In the evening she went, and on the morrow she returned into the second house of the women, to the custody of Shaashgaz, the king's chamberlain, which kept the concubines: she came in unto the king no more, except the king delighted in her, and that she were called by name.*
> *¹⁵ Now when the turn of Esther, the daughter of Abihail the uncle of Mordecai, who had taken her for his daughter, was come to go in unto the king, she required nothing but what Hegai the king's chamberlain, the keeper of the women, appointed. And Esther obtained favour in the sight of all them that looked upon her.*
> *¹⁶ So Esther was taken unto king Ahasuerus into his house royal in the tenth month, which is the month Tebeth, in the seventh year of his reign.*
> *¹⁷ And the king loved Esther above all the women, and she obtained grace and favour in his sight more than all the virgins; so that he set*

the royal crown upon her head, and made her queen instead of Vashti.

Esther 2:12-17

This is not to say that the preparation of the outward should exceed that of the heart. They are both important. Again, remember the story of the beggar thrown out in the gospel of Matthew. He was thrown out because of his raiment.

> ¹ And Jesus answered and spake unto them again by parables, and said,
> ² The kingdom of heaven is like unto a certain king, which made a marriage for his son,
> ³ And sent forth his servants to call them that were bidden to the wedding: and they would not come.
> ⁴ Again, he sent forth other servants, saying, Tell them which are bidden, Behold, I have prepared my dinner: my oxen and my fatlings are killed, and all things are ready: come unto the marriage.
> ⁵ But they made light of it, and went their ways, one to his farm, another to his merchandise:
> ⁶ And the remnant took his servants, and entreated them spitefully, and slew them.
> ⁷ But when the king heard thereof, he was wroth: and he sent forth his armies, and destroyed those murderers, and burned up their city.
> ⁸ Then saith he to his servants, The wedding is ready, but they which were bidden were not worthy.
> ⁹ Go ye therefore into the highways, and as many as ye shall find, bid to the marriage.
> ¹⁰ So those servants went out into the highways, and gathered together all as many as they found, both bad and good: and the wedding was furnished with guests.
> ¹¹ And when the king came in to see the guests, he saw there a man which had not on a wedding garment:
> ¹² And he saith unto him, Friend, how camest thou in hither not having a wedding garment? And he was speechless.
> ¹³ Then said the king to the servants, Bind him hand and foot, and take him away, and cast him into outer darkness, there shall be weeping and gnashing of teeth.

Qualifying for the Knowledge

¹⁴ *For many are called, but few are chosen.*

Matthew 22:1-14

Despising the outward appearance is not wise. Dressing right may have a bigger impact than you think and dressing right does not have to mean dress expensive.

As believers, How have we been prepared to stand in the presence of the King of kings? Christ has made a way for us by shedding His blood. Look at what Apostle Paul had to say.

> ¹¹ *But [that appointed time came] when Christ (the Messiah) appeared as a High Priest of the better things that have come and are to come. [Then] through the greater and more perfect tabernacle not made with [human] hands, that is, not a part of this material creation,*
> ¹² *He went once for all into the [Holy of] Holies [of heaven], not by virtue of the blood of goats and calves [by which to make reconciliation between God and man], but His own blood, having found and secured a complete redemption (an everlasting release for us).*
> ¹³ *For if [the mere] sprinkling of unholy and defiled persons with blood of goats and bulls and with the ashes of a burnt heifer is sufficient for the purification of the body,*
> ¹⁴ *How much more surely shall the blood of Christ, Who by virtue of [His] eternal Spirit [His own preexistent [b]divine personality] has offered Himself as an unblemished sacrifice to God, purify our consciences from dead works and lifeless observances to serve the [ever] living God?*
> ¹⁵ *[Christ, the Messiah] is therefore the Negotiator and Mediator of an [entirely] new agreement (testament, covenant), so that those who are called and offered it may receive the fulfillment of the promised everlasting inheritance--since a death has taken place which rescues and delivers and redeems them from the transgressions committed under the [old] first agreement.*

Hebrews 9:11-15 (AMP)

Christ has opened a new and living way for us to enter into the King's presence. The great news is that we are not entering into a tarbernacle made with hands, we are entering into the holiest place of all. Praise God! Believing this fact and walking in the reality of it will bring a bounce to our steps. We can now enter into His presence without a consciousness of sin.

Glory to God!.

Chapter Key Points

Without a promise from above, there is no guarantee of a manifestation

The seed of God makes you more than spiritual, it makes you a spirit

Favour should not be taken lightly. It could be the difference between toiling without result and productivity without tears

The heart of a man is not designed to express affectionate love to more than one woman at the same time

Diligence means chipping at the challenge a little at a time until a finished and desirable outcome is reached

4

Operating in Knowledge

A man who has a tool and does not know how to use it is no better than a man without the tool. Having knowledge and not operating or utilising the knowledge still equals zero productivity. It is one thing to possess a tool, it is another thing to know how to use the tool effectively. I remember reading the response of a man of God when asked about one of the things he admired most in his mentor, the great healing evangelist Oral Roberts. He said, *"he uses his faith like a tool"*. A lot of believers are defeated in life, not because they do not have the authority to overcome the devil, but because they do not know how to use the authority they already possess.

Paul the Apostle talked about people who were ever learning and never able to get to the tipping point for action.

> [7] *Ever learning, and never able to come to the knowledge of the truth.*
>
> 2 Timothy 3:7

The Amplified Bible's rendition is more explosive and I hope you realise that even though it says women, it still applies to men.

> ⁷ *[These weak women will listen to anybody who will teach them]; they are forever inquiring and getting information, but are never able to arrive at a recognition and knowledge of the Truth.*
>
> 2 Timothy 3:7 (AMP)

Now, there is a time for everything. A time for preparation and a time for action. We have prepared long enough, now we need to act. The devil has gained enough ground, now it is time for us to take back what rightfully belongs to us. If the lack of knowledge destroys, the presence of it should give life. You are reading this book because of a quest for knowledge. For some of you, the seeds of knowledge you are picking from this book is enough for you to start making an impact right away.

> ² *For unto us was the gospel preached, as well as unto them: but the word preached did not profit them, not being mixed with faith in them that heard it.*
>
> Hebrews 4:2

What does it mean to "*mix with faith*". This means getting to a point where the Word of God you hear brings your knowledge and understanding to the tipping point that propels you to action. The Amplified Bible's description of *Hebrews 4:2* is wonderful.

> ² *For indeed we have had the glad tidings [Gospel of God] proclaimed to us just as truly as they [the Israelites of old did when the good news of deliverance from bondage came to them]; but the message they heard did not benefit them, because it was not mixed with faith (with the leaning of the entire personality on God in absolute trust and confidence in His power, wisdom, and goodness) by those who heard it; neither were they united in faith with the ones [Joshua and Caleb]*

who heard (did believe).

Hebrews 4:2 (AMP)

The longer it takes you to act on a revelation, the less its potency in your life. This is not because the word of God losses potency but you lose the spiritual energy the revelation imparted. This is part of the principle Jesus was teaching in the parable of the sower in *Mark 4:1-20*.

One of the fundamental truths we need to embrace as we start walking in the light of this truth about knowledge is the fact that the knowledge comes from God. God is pouring out this type of knowledge for the distinguishing and elevation of believers in the Church because He wants our light to shine and confound the wisdom of the world. This sort of knowledge can only come through the presence of a spirit or divine being in man.

> *⁸ But there is a spirit in man: and the inspiration of the Almighty giveth them understanding.*

Job 32:8

The prophet Isaiah also describes the source of this type of knowledge.

> *¹ And there shall come forth a rod out of the stem of Jesse, and a Branch shall grow out of his roots:*
> *² AND THE SPIRIT OF THE LORD SHALL REST UPON HIM, the spirit of wisdom and understanding, the spirit of counsel and might, THE SPIRIT OF KNOWLEDGE and of the fear of the LORD;*
> *³ And shall make him of quick understanding in the fear of the LORD: and he shall not judge after the sight of his eyes, neither reprove after the hearing of his ears:*

Isaiah 11:1-3

It is interesting that Nebu-chad-nez'-zar was not looking for children that only had knowledge. He was looking for children that were *cunning in knowledge,* signifying he was after children who knew how to use facts skillfully. Every Christian walking in the light of the knowledge of God should be an intellectual giant that demonstrates the spirit of a sound-mind.

Looking further into the story, we see how the king intended the Hebrew boys to acquire the knowledge. They were going to attend a three year educational program before they could function in the Babylonian system.

> *4 children in whom was no blemish, but well favoured, and skilful in all wisdom, and cunning in knowledge, and understanding science, and such as had ability in them to stand in the king's palace, and WHOM THEY MIGHT TEACH THE LEARNING AND THE TONGUE OF THE CHALDEANS.*
> *5 And the king appointed them a daily provision of the king's meat, and of the wine which he drank: SO NOURISHING THEM THREE YEARS, that at the end thereof they might stand before the king*
>
> Daniel 1:4-5

Apostle Paul describes a similar process of training and development in his letter to the Galatians.

> *1 Now I say, That the heir, as long as he is a child, differeth nothing from a servant, though he be lord of all;*
> *2 But IS UNDER TUTORS AND GOVERNORS UNTIL THE TIME APPOINTED OF THE FATHER.*
> *3 Even so we, when we were children, were in bondage under the elements of the world:*
> *4 But when the fulness of the time was come, God sent forth his Son, made of a woman, made under the law,*
>
> Galatians 4:1-4

For someone reading this book, your fullness of time has come, go and shine and manifest your glory. Let the grace for Sonship begin to manifest in you from this day forward.

Let's us look at some of the traits necessary for operating

in knowledge successfully. For example, we have the story of a woman in the New Testament that had an amazing encounter with Jesus. While the story is one of a woman seeking help for her daughter suffering under the oppression of the devil, there is a vital fact that makes her story very relevant here. Circumstances over which she had no control put her in a position of disqualification. However something else she had qualified her. Her faith.

Faith

Is it possible to talk about getting anything from God without talking about faith? The fact that you decide to go to God is itself an act of faith. Your decision to go to God means you believe He exists. Believing in God means you believe in what you cannot see.

> [21] Then Jesus went thence, and departed into the coasts of Tyre and Sidon.
> [22] And, behold, a woman of Canaan came out of the same coasts, and cried unto him, saying, Have mercy on me, O Lord, thou son of David; my daughter is grievously vexed with a devil.
> [23] But he answered her not a word. And his disciples came and besought him, saying, Send her away; for she crieth after us.
> [24] But he answered and said, I am not sent but unto the lost sheep of the house of Israel.
> [25] Then came she and worshipped him, saying, Lord, help me.
> [26] But he answered and said, It is not meet to take the children's bread, and to cast it to dogs.
> [27] And she said, Truth, Lord: yet the dogs eat of the crumbs which fall from their masters' table.
> [28] Then Jesus answered and said unto her, O woman, great is thy faith: be it unto thee even as thou wilt. And her daughter was made whole from that very hour.
>
> *Matthew 15:21-28*

Notice Jesus commended this woman's faith and even

called it great faith. Why did Jesus call it great faith?

> ²⁸ *Then Jesus answered and said unto her, O woman, great is thy faith: be it unto thee even as thou wilt. And her daughter was made whole from that very hour.*
>
> Matthew 15:21-28

This woman must have built up her faith in Jesus from the words she heard of Him prior to the encounter. She even called Him *thou Son of David* to demonstrate the fact that she knew something about the person she was calling. Being born to Nigerian parents, I have quite a few names. Most people know me as Akin but there are a few names I get called that stops me in my tracks. It tells me the person calling me knows me, knows my family and must be close enough to know what my father calls me. My response to the person calling me is then no longer just a casual response but a response based on the relationship the person calling me has with my family.

Remember, faith comes by hearing the Word of God (*Romans 10:17*). You cannot go to God unless you have heard about Him and you cannot hear about Him if someone has not spoken about Him to you. People who take time to find out about God always seems to have great faith. This story shows us one of the greatest characteristics of faith. Let us ask the question again, what about this woman did Jesus see to make Him call her faith *great*?

> ²⁷ *And she said, Truth, Lord: yet the dogs eat of the crumbs which fall from their masters' table.*
> ²⁸ *Then Jesus answered and said unto her, O woman, great is thy faith: be it unto thee even as thou wilt. And her daughter was made whole from that very hour.*
>
> Matthew 15:27-28

I believe it was her actions that were followed the words

coming out of her mouth. She believed Jesus was the Son of David and not just any Rabbi. The spirit of faith that says, *I believe, therefore I speak* (2 Corinthians 4:13) was in operation in her. Her faith had actions. She believed in the power of the spoken word to effect change in her circumstances. Notice that this account by Matthew does not explicitly state that the daughter was there with her when she talked to Jesus. Also, Jesus did not specifically address the daughter or the devils that troubled her. When you walk in the dimension of great faith, the results you obtain are consistent with the expectation you had prior to acting in faith. What was her expectation? She wanted her daughter to be healed of the devil that vexed her.

The power of God only produces to the level of revelation of the word of God you have. (*3 John 1:2*). You cannot be transformed beyond your revelation (*Romans 12:1-2*). The power of God is limited by what your mind contains. It is the depth of your revelation that determines the height of your achievement.

The account of Mark however confirms that the daughter was not with the woman at the time this conversation with Jesus was taking place.

> *²⁹ And he said unto her, For this saying go thy way; the devil is gone out of thy daughter.*
> *³⁰ And when she was come to her house, she found the devil gone out, and her daughter laid upon the bed.*
>
> *Mark 7:29-30*

Every promise we will receive from God must be by faith. This means one of the actions we must engage in, in order to obtain a good report (*Hebrews 11:2*) must include the utterance of words that have been revealed to us by the Holy Spirit.

For by the confession of the mouth, salvation comes (Romans 10:8-10)

> *⁸ But what saith it? The word is nigh thee, even in thy mouth, and in thy heart: that is, the word of faith, which we preach;*
> *⁹ That if thou shalt confess with thy mouth the Lord Jesus, and shalt believe in thine heart that God hath raised him from the dead, thou shalt be saved.*
> *¹⁰ For with the heart man believeth unto righteousness; and with the mouth confession is made unto salvation.*
>
> Romans 10:8-10

The order ordained by God for getting results by faith is firstly to believe *(have confidence or conviction in the authority of the spoken Word to effect the change desired)* in the heart then secondly, speak repeatedly with the mouth, the things believed in the heart irrespective of the natural circumstances.

Look at what Jesus says in the gospel of Mark.

> *²² And Jesus answering saith unto them, Have faith in God.*
> *²³ For verily I say unto you, That whosoever shall say unto this mountain, Be thou removed, and be thou cast into the sea; and shall not doubt in his heart, but shall believe that those things which he saith shall come to pass; he shall have whatsoever he saith.*
> *²⁴ Therefore I say unto you, What things soever ye desire, when ye pray, believe that ye receive them, and ye shall have them.*
>
> Mark 11:22-24

Notice the number of times the words *"say"* and *"saith"* is used in *verse 23*. Notice it does not say you will have what you believe, it says *"he shall have whatsoever he saith"*. The potency of the power of God is released by the spoken word. There is nothing God created that was not preceded with Him saying something.

Persistence

Despite the fact that this woman had been ignored, she persisted. She did not give up. The people who were close enough to the Master even formed a coalition against her. This is one of the reasons we are instructed in the Bible to never put our trust in the arm of flesh because this will always fail. (Jeremiah 17:5)

> [23] But he answered her not a word. And his disciples came and besought him, saying, Send her away; for she crieth after us.
>
> Matthew 15:23

As if this first obstacle was not enough, when she eventually got to the Master, she was given a reason for why she did not qualify for what she desired.

> [24] But he answered and said, I am not sent but unto the lost sheep of the house of Israel.
>
> Matthew 15:24

This reason given also represented a significant challenge, one that could not be easily overcome by natural means. The response was really saying she did not qualify for her request because of her race. How do you change such a restriction? No amount of skin lighting cream, hair attachment and relaxing cream will ever make a black man a white man. Neither can a white man suddenly become Asian because of changes made to the external. I hope you understand the gravity of the response from Jesus.

This reason notwithstanding, the woman who is obviously of quick understanding and full of wits uses the same analogy of dogs and gives us one of the most exciting insights into how to overcome adversity and make contrary situations work in our favour.

> [27] And she said, Truth, Lord: yet the dogs eat of the crumbs which fall from their masters' table.
>
> Matthew 15:27

She refers to the healing of her demon possessed daughter as crumbs. In other words, the real substance that belonged to the children was divine health but the crumbs of *healing* belonged to the foreigners. She said *"Truth Lord"*. What did this mean? She was aware that at the time she was making her request, it was not yet the appointed time for her to be able to claim the blessing of salvation. The gospel had not yet been preached to the Greeks and Jesus had not yet died on the cross for all. She was ready with an answer to cast down every thought of disqualification. She could easily have said, Well it is Jesus, He knows the will of God. It is probably not the will of God for me. Was Jesus right? Yes. Could He resist responding to a faith request? No.

I believe a lot of people miss out on the blessing of God because of lack of persistence, listening to the crowd as your primary source of direction and offences in the heart. We need to learn to dissolve doubts and cast down imaginations contrary to the will of God for our lives. There is a right way and a wrong way to make a request. The fact that someone gets *"No"* as an answer is not evidence of the unwillingness of the giver to give.

Persistence is the characteristic that makes one *"hold-on"* almost to the point of stubbornness or disregard. It means not letting go and not taking *"no"* for an answer. The battle is not over until the answer is the right answer as indicated in the promise of God backing the believer. This is why it is important for every Believer to make sure every request made to God is based on a promise.

Look at an example in the story of the Shunnammite

woman in the Old Testatment

> ²² And she called unto her husband, and said, Send me, I pray thee, one of the young men, and one of the asses, that I may run to the man of God, and come again.
> ²³ And he said, Wherefore wilt thou go to him to day? it is neither new moon, nor sabbath. And she said, It shall be well.
> ²⁴ Then she saddled an ass, and said to her servant, Drive, and go forward; slack not thy riding for me, except I bid thee.
> ²⁵ So she went and came unto the man of God to mount Carmel. And it came to pass, when the man of God saw her afar off, that he said to Gehazi his servant, Behold, yonder is that Shunammite:
> ²⁶ Run now, I pray thee, to meet her, and say unto her, Is it well with thee? is it well with thy husband? is it well with the child? And she answered, It is well:
> ²⁷ And when she came to the man of God to the hill, she caught him by the feet: but Gehazi came near to thrust her away. And the man of God said, Let her alone; for her soul is vexed within her: and the LORD hath hid it from me, and hath not told me.
> ²⁸ Then she said, Did I desire a son of my lord? did I not say, Do not deceive me?
> ²⁹ Then he said to Gehazi, Gird up thy loins, and take my staff in thine hand, and go thy way: if thou meet any man, salute him not; and if any salute thee, answer him not again: and lay my staff upon the face of the child.
> ³⁰ And the mother of the child said, As the LORD liveth, and as thy soul liveth, I will not leave thee. And he arose, and followed her.
> ³¹ And Gehazi passed on before them, and laid the staff upon the face of the child; but there was neither voice, nor hearing. Wherefore he went again to meet him, and told him, saying, The child is not awaked.
>
> *2 Kings 4:22-31*

Sometimes, we are too dignified to take this tenacious approach in holding fast to God until our answers become a reality. This woman at first, could have accepted the death of her son as an irreversible situation but she pursued the man of God. Secondly, she could have been offended and given up when Gehazi pushed her away in the presence of the man of God. Remember, she was a great woman.

Thirdly she could have accepted Gehazi going with the staff for which nothing would have happened. (*verse 31*) This situation was different, even Elisha was surprised that God had not shown him what the problem was.

> ²⁷ And when she came to the man of God to the hill, she caught him by the feet: but Gehazi came near to thrust her away. And the man of God said, Let her alone; for her soul is vexed within her: and the LORD hath hid it from me, and hath not told me.
>
> 2 Kings 4:27

Even when Elisha got there, the situation still seemed to be a *"difficult"* situation but Elisha continued until he got the desired result.

> ³³ He went in therefore, and shut the door upon them twain, and prayed unto the LORD.
> ³⁴ And he went up, and lay upon the child, and put his mouth upon his mouth, and his eyes upon his eyes, and his hands upon his hands: and stretched himself upon the child; and the flesh of the child waxed warm.
> ³⁵ Then he returned, and walked in the house to and fro; and went up, and stretched himself upon him: and the child sneezed seven times, and the child opened his eyes.
> ³⁶ And he called Gehazi, and said, Call this Shunammite. So he called her. And when she was come in unto him, he said, Take up thy son.
> ³⁷ Then she went in, and fell at his feet, and bowed herself to the ground, and took up her son, and went out.
>
> 2 Kings 4:33-37

It was first the staff that had been laid on the child with nothing happening, it could have been concluded at that point that it was not the will of God for the child to rise. Then it was Elisha praying from the depths of his soul for an answer from God. He goes to the child but his results are only marginal. Elisha could have given up here. Elisha walks to and fro in the house as though he was searching for an answer. This time, the child sneezed and opened his eyes.

Persistence keeps us in the battle until the result favours us. We are not a company of failures. We are possessors of the promise with access to the blessing of Abraham flowing through Isaac and Jacob to Jesus and to us.

Isaac, yet another patriarch, demonstrated such tenacity. He continued digging the well until he got the inheritance that belonged to him as these were wells dug in the days of Abraham

> [17] And Isaac departed thence, and pitched his tent in the valley of Gerar, and dwelt there.
> [18] And Isaac digged again the wells of water, which they had digged in the days of Abraham his father; for the Philistines had stopped them after the death of Abraham: and he called their names after the names by which his father had called them.
> [19] And Isaac's servants digged in the valley, and found there a well of springing water.
> [20] And the herdmen of Gerar did strive with Isaac's herdmen, saying, The water is ours: and he called the name of the well Esek; because they strove with him.
> [21] And they digged another well, and strove for that also: and he called the name of it Sitnah.
> [22] And he removed from thence, and digged another well; and for that they strove not: and he called the name of it Rehoboth; and he said, For now the LORD hath made room for us, and we shall be fruitful in the land.
>
> *Genesis 26:17-22*

These wells of Abraham that were blocked are still being unblocked by faith. Isaac did not get a result until the third time, yet he stayed with the vision until the vision brought forth a stream of water. Stay with your vision, do not quit. God will surely show up for you. If Isaac did not quit and the Shummanite woman did not quit and the Greek woman did not quit. Why should you quit? If I was going to include your story as one of these ones highlighted here, what would it be? How would it have ended?

Courage

Courage is the combination of a state of mind and physical demeanour that causes a person to face a situation as though the possibility of a negative or unwanted outcome does not exist. It is behaving authoritatively in a situation even though the outcome desired depends on the activation of supernatural forces which are unseen to the natural eyes. Courage is the state of mind in which thought of loss or possibility of failure is completely eliminated because of our trust in the power of the God that is available to us. It causes one to exhibit an appearance of strength. Many times in scriptures, we notice that this courageous demeanour was always required when the people of God faced challenges that looked insurmountable. Before the children of Israel got to the promised land, Moses sent spies to spy the land and Moses instructs them to be of good courage.

> [17] And Moses sent them to spy out the land of Canaan, and said unto them, Get you up this way southward, and go up into the mountain: [18] And see the land, what it is, and the people that dwelleth therein, whether they be strong or weak, few or many;
> [19] And what the land is that they dwell in, whether it be good or bad; and what cities they be that they dwell in, whether in tents, or in strong holds;
> [20] And what the land is, whether it be fat or lean, whether there be wood therein, or not. **AND BE YE OF GOOD COURAGE, AND BRING OF THE FRUIT OF THE LAND.** Now the time was the time of the firstripe grapes.
>
> Numbers 13:17-20

Though the Canaanites possessed what the children of Israel wanted, the spies were not to present themselves as second class citizens because God had promised them the Land. As Moses said, we need to be of good courage. Christ has already paid the price for our inheritance. All things are now accessible to us.

These spies went out and came back but we see that though twelve men went out to spy the land, it seems only two really had good courage. These ten spies magnified everything and everyone in the land until it became a stumbling block to them.

> *²⁶ And they went and came to Moses, and to Aaron, and to all the congregation of the children of Israel, unto the wilderness of Paran, to Kadesh; and brought back word unto them, and unto all the congregation, and shewed them the fruit of the land.*
> *²⁷ And they told him, and said, We came unto the land whither thou sentest us, and surely it floweth with milk and honey; and this is the fruit of it.*
> *²⁸ Nevertheless the people be strong that dwell in the land, and the cities are walled, and very great: and moreover we saw the children of Anak there.*
> *²⁹ The Amalekites dwell in the land of the south: and the Hittites, and the Jebusites, and the Amorites, dwell in the mountains: and the Canaanites dwell by the sea, and by the coast of Jordan.*
> *³⁰ And Caleb stilled the people before Moses, and said, Let us go up at once, and possess it; for we are well able to overcome it.*
> *³¹ But the men that went up with him said, We be not able to go up against the people; for they are stronger than we.*
> *³² And they brought up an evil report of the land which they had searched unto the children of Israel, saying, The land, through which we have gone to search it, is a land that eateth up the inhabitants thereof; and all the people that we saw in it are men of a great stature.*
> *³³ And there we saw the giants, the sons of Anak, which come of the giants: and we were in our own sight as grasshoppers, and so we were in their sight.*
>
> Numbers 13:26-33

Every negative situation magnified in this way becomes a stumbling block. These same situations are seen as a stepping stone in the eyes of the courageous ones. Had Joshua and Caleb not been courageous, these ten spies could have prolonged the time of entry into the promise of God. The forces of the earth respond to you based on the way you perceive yourself. You cannot have fear on the inside and people outside see courage. The state of your heart has a voice.

> [33] And there we saw the giants, the sons of Anak, which come of the giants: and we were in our own sight as grasshoppers, and so we were in their sight.
>
> *Numbers 13:26-33*

These spies were in their own sights as grasshoppers. At least, ten of them were. Every time you look to the natural circumstances as your sole source of information for decision making, the grasshopper mentality gains strength. However, when courage is employed, every mountain is surmountable. The power of the endless life that resides in the believer makes all things possible to him. Look at the story of Gideon. The percentage of those who were afraid was not too dissimilar to the days of Joshua and Caleb in the days of the spies.

Courage is what separates the actors from the spectators. Courageous people have a possibility mentality. Have you realised that most of the time, spectators always know better than actors, especially in games like football, yet they never go near the playing field. Courageous people see why things can be done and have answers to obstacles.

> [1] Then Jerubbaal, who is Gideon, and all the people that were with him, rose up early, and pitched beside the well of Harod: so that the host of the Midianites were on the north side of them, by the hill of Moreh, in the valley.
> [2] And the LORD said unto Gideon, The people that are with thee are too many for me to give the Midianites into their hands, lest Israel

vaunt themselves against me, saying, Mine own hand hath saved me.
³ Now therefore go to, proclaim in the ears of the people, saying,
WHOSOEVER IS FEARFUL AND AFRAID, LET HIM RETURN AND DEPART EARLY FROM MOUNT GILEAD. *And there returned of the people twenty and two thousand; and there remained ten thousand.*

Judges 7:1-3

Of the thirty-two thousand that gathered, only ten thousand had courage. Had these twenty-two thousand gone to battle with Gideon, they would have broken rank in the heat of the battle and brought defeat to the people of God. True fighters are courageous men with unwavering faith in the power of God to bring deliverance.

³² And what shall I more say? for the time would fail me to tell of Gedeon, and of Barak, and of Samson, and of Jephthae; of David also, and Samuel, and of the prophets:
³³ Who through faith subdued kingdoms, wrought righteousness, obtained promises, stopped the mouths of lions.
³⁴ Quenched the violence of fire, escaped the edge of the sword, out of weakness were made strong, waxed valiant in fight, turned to flight the armies of the aliens.
³⁵ Women received their dead raised to life again: and others were tortured, not accepting deliverance; that they might obtain a better resurrection:

Hebrews 11:32-35

Let us look at courage in these Hebrew boys walking in this unstoppable force of courage that attracted the attention of Heaven.

¹⁴ Nebuchadnezzar spake and said unto them, Is it true, O Shadrach, Meshach, and Abednego, do not ye serve my gods, nor worship the golden image which I have set up?
¹⁵ Now if ye be ready that at what time ye hear the sound of the cornet, flute, harp, sackbut, psaltery, and dulcimer, and all kinds of musick, ye fall down and worship the image which I have made; well: but if ye worship not, ye shall be cast the same hour into the midst of a burning fiery furnace; and who is that God that shall deliver you out

of my hands?

¹⁶ Shadrach, Meshach, and Abednego, answered and said to the king, O Nebuchadnezzar, we are not careful to answer thee in this matter.

¹⁷ If it be so, our God whom we serve is able to deliver us from the burning fiery furnace, and he will deliver us out of thine hand, O king.

¹⁸ But if not, be it known unto thee, O king, that we will not serve thy gods, nor worship the golden image which thou hast set up.

¹⁹ Then was Nebuchadnezzar full of fury, and the form of his visage was changed against Shadrach, Meshach, and Abednego: therefore he spake, and commanded that they should heat the furnace one seven times more than it was wont to be heated.

²⁰ And he commanded the most mighty men that were in his army to bind Shadrach, Meshach, and Abednego, and to cast them into the burning fiery furnace.

²¹ Then these men were bound in their coats, their hosen, and their hats, and their other garments, and were cast into the midst of the burning fiery furnace.

²² Therefore because the king's commandment was urgent, and the furnace exceeding hot, the flames of the fire slew those men that took up Shadrach, Meshach, and Abednego.

²³ And these three men, Shadrach, Meshach, and Abednego, fell down bound into the midst of the burning fiery furnace.

²⁴Then Nebuchadnezzar the king was astonished, and rose up in haste, and spake, and said unto his counsellors, Did not we cast three men bound into the midst of the fire? They answered and said unto the king, True, O king.

²⁵ He answered and said, Lo, I see four men loose, walking in the midst of the fire, and they have no hurt; and the form of the fourth is like the Son of God.

Daniel 3:14-25

It takes courage to answer a king like they did. Without this courage, the elevation would not have come.

For someone reading this book, the last thing needed for you is courage. Get up now and do what the Lord has placed in your heart. Be free from the spirit of fear and walk into your liberty in Jesus Name.

Operating in Knowledge

The work of faith is usually greater than what the mind can comprehend and always requires courage. For most people, the promise of greatness is received when the physical circumstances do not make the person receiving the promise look great. God uses this pattern to make sure it is of faith otherwise we will believe in our own strength.

> ² *And the LORD said unto Gideon, The people that are with thee are too many for me to give the Midianites into their hands,* **LEST ISRAEL VAUNT THEMSELVES AGAINST ME, SAYING, MINE OWN HAND HATH SAVED ME.*
>
> *Judges 7:2*

Joshua is another patriarch that was in a similar situation of attempting something that was greater than him and to whom God told to be courageous.

> ¹ *Now after the death of Moses the servant of the LORD it came to pass, that the LORD spake unto Joshua the son of Nun, Moses' minister, saying,*
> ² *Moses my servant is dead; now therefore arise, go over this Jordan, thou, and all this people, unto the land which I do give to them, even to the children of Israel.*
> ³ *Every place that the sole of your foot shall tread upon, that have I given unto you, as I said unto Moses.*
> ⁴ *From the wilderness and this Lebanon even unto the great river, the river Euphrates, all the land of the Hittites, and unto the great sea toward the going down of the sun, shall be your coast.*
> ⁵ *There shall not any man be able to stand before thee all the days of thy life: as I was with Moses, so I will be with thee: I will not fail thee, nor forsake thee.*
> ⁶ **BE STRONG AND OF A GOOD COURAGE:** *for unto this people shalt thou divide for an inheritance the land, which I sware unto their fathers to give them.*
> ⁷ **ONLY BE THOU STRONG AND VERY COURAGEOUS,** *that thou mayest observe to do according to all the law, which Moses my servant commanded thee: turn not from it to the right hand or to the left, that thou mayest prosper withersoever thou goest.*
> ⁸ *This book of the law shall not depart out of thy mouth; but thou*

> *shalt meditate therein day and night, that thou mayest observe to do according to all that is written therein: for then thou shalt make thy way prosperous, and then thou shalt have good success.*
> *⁹ Have not I commanded thee?* **BE STRONG AND OF A GOOD COURAGE; BE NOT AFRAID,** *neither be thou dismayed: for the LORD thy God is with thee whithersoever thou goest.*
>
> Joshua 1:1-9

See the number of times God told Joshua to be courageous for this great assignment God was committing into his hands. Whatever assignment God has given you is achievable irrespective of your background and experiences in life. The only limitations that exist are the ones you have imposed yourself.

Courage is something you put on as someone puts on a cloak. It is the outward appearance of your inward strength and is always based on a promise from God.

Chapter Key Points

Having knowledge and not operating or utilising the knowledge still equals zero productivity

If the lack of knowledge destroys, the presence of it should give life

The longer it takes to act on a revelation, the less its potency in your life. This is not because the Word of God losses potency but you lose the spiritual energy the word imparted

Every Christian walking in the light of the knowledge of God should be an intellectual giant

It is the depth of your revelation that determines the height of your achievement

Courage is the state of mind in which thought of loss or possibility of failure is completely eliminated

5

The Rewards of Knowledge

*I*t took the Hebrew boys only ten days for the evidence of what they were engaged in to start to show. But do not be deceived, it must have taken more than ten days for them to get to a point where they were sure that their faith was going to work. If we constantly stay in the presence of God and His Word, our profiting will appear unto all. Operating in knowledge has rewards because God is a rewarder of those who diligently seek him. God does not tell us to do something just to prove a point. He tells us to do things because it is the right thing to do. Knowledge has tangible benefits. You cannot gain the right knowledge inside without it being obvious on the outside but it takes more than just *knowing* for knowledge to be active. Just knowing makes you a reference point but getting results with knowledge makes you an achiever.

Knowledge has many rewards that we could highlight but let us look at a some that, according to the Bible, are a direct product of knowledge.

Access to divine nature

Being born-again gives us access to eternal life but how exactly does the life come? Knowledge brings us into oneness with the life and nature of God. Godly knowledge changes the person before it changes the environment. Being driven by the external is walking by sight. For the spiritual man, the manifestation on the outside is only a sign of what is going on in the heart. Being spirits, our worlds are framed by our words. We walk by faith and not by sight and we know that what we see was made from what we do not see. Therefore Godly knowledge enlarges the spirit man first.

Peter in his first epistle, gives us some insight into how knowledge gives us access to divine nature. Expanding the *divine nature* in Peter's epistle, we get a better understanding of what Peter was talking about concerning this nature. Knowledge makes us aware of the promises that open up the door of this divine nature to us.

> ³ *According as his divine power hath given unto us all things that pertain unto life and godliness, THROUGH THE KNOWLEDGE of him that hath called us to glory and virtue:*
> ⁴ *Whereby are given unto us exceeding great and precious promises: that by these ye might be PARTAKERS OF THE DIVINE NATURE (puff, breath or implant that has the native disposition to grow through expansion or swelling up), having escaped the corruption that is in the world through lust*
>
> *2 Peter 1:3-4*

In the beginning when God created Adam, God made him a living soul by breathing into him. This was the point at which this *"puff"* representing the nature of God came into Adam.

> ⁷ *And the LORD God formed man of the dust of the ground, and breathed into his nostrils the breath of life; and man became a living soul.*
>
> Genesis 2:7

Adam was lifeless without this *"puff"* that gave life to the body made from the dust of the ground. This means the *"puff"* came into him and inflated him as air inflates a balloon causing a soul and spirit to be deposited in the body of dust. This *"puff"* swells and expands until it fills its container with intellect and inspiration and the container begins to exhibit characteristics of the *"puff"*.

In Ezekiel 37, Ezekiel was asked if the dry bones could live? I had read and heard this story preached a number of times but recently, the Holy Spirit showed me that this was a two part prophecy and we could miss a lot by not looking at the second part.

The first prophecy dealt with creating a form. This was about bones coming together, and flesh covering the bones but notice verse 8. It says *"...but there was no breath in them"*

> ¹ *The hand of the LORD was upon me, and carried me out in the spirit of the LORD, and set me down in the midst of the valley which was full of bones,*
> ² *And caused me to pass by them round about: and, behold, there were very many in the open valley; and, lo, they were very dry.*
> ³ *And he said unto me, Son of man, can these bones live? And I answered, O Lord GOD, thou knowest.*
> ⁴ *Again he said unto me, Prophesy upon these bones, and say unto them, O ye dry bones, hear the word of the LORD.*
> ⁵ *Thus saith the Lord GOD unto these bones; Behold, I will cause breath to enter into you, and ye shall live:*
> ⁶ *And I will lay sinews upon you, and will bring up flesh upon you, and cover you with skin, and put breath in you, and ye shall live; and ye shall know that I am the LORD.*
> ⁷ *So I prophesied as I was commanded: and as I prophesied, there was*

a noise, and behold a shaking, and the bones came together, bone to his bone.
⁸ And when I beheld, lo, the sinews and the flesh came up upon them, and the skin covered them above: but there was no breath in them.
⁹ Then said he unto me, Prophesy unto the wind, prophesy, son of man, and say to the wind, Thus saith the Lord GOD; Come from the four winds, O breath, and breathe upon these slain, that they may live.
¹⁰ So I prophesied as he commanded me, and the breath came into them, and they lived, and stood up upon their feet, an exceeding great army.

Ezekiel 37:1-10

No breath? Was it not God that told Ezekiel to prophesy? The bones came together, flesh came on the bones yet here was no life. It took the second prophecy (*verse 10*) for breath to come into the bodies and for them to live. What is my point here? More often than not, God's "breath" requires a "form" to inhabit. You may have had an idea for so long and it may seem like your prayers concerning the idea are not being answered. That may just be the problem, *it is an idea*. You have not created a form for that idea and the breath of God has nothing to infuse. For others, they have created the form by the prophetic word but have not asked God for the prophetic word to deliver the breath that causes things to come alive. I believe God is saying to you, prophesy again and that thing you desire, that door that seems like an unbreakable barrier, that age old issue will hear the voice of the Son of God and live.

The psalmist in *Psalm 82:6* and John in *John 10:34-35*, refers to the ones to whom the word of God came as gods.

⁶ I have said, Ye are gods; and all of you are children of the most High.

Psalm 82:6

³⁴ Jesus answered them, Is it not written in your law, I said, Ye are gods?
³⁵ If he called them gods, unto whom the word of God came, and the

scripture cannot be broken;
³⁶ Say ye of him, whom the Father hath sanctified, and sent into the world, Thou blasphemest; because I said, I am the Son of God?

John 10:34-36

Did you notice those that were called gods? Read *verse 35* again. Those unto whom the word of God came! When God wanted to heal people in the Old Testamant, what did He do? *Psalm 107:20* says *"He sent His Word and healed them"*. When the Word of God came, their physical bodies were changed into whatever the Word of God contained which includes healing. This is why I say, the area in which you experience weakness is usually the area in which the Word of God has not become a reality in your life. If you let the Word of God have its full way and grow to maturity in any area of your life, you will manifest *God-like* characteristics in that area.

This breath is what makes all the difference in the Believer's walk of victory. Everyone that walks and lives under the influence of this breath exhibits *"God-like"* characteristics. Let us look at one such example in the life of Jesus. When Jesus walked in this level of knowledge, the people were shocked. It was *"God like"* authority given to men.

> ³ And they come unto him, bringing one sick of the palsy, which was borne of four.
> ⁴ And when they could not come nigh unto him for the press, they uncovered the roof where he was: and when they had broken it up, they let down the bed wherein the sick of the palsy lay.
> ⁵ When Jesus saw their faith, he said unto the sick of the palsy, Son, thy sins be forgiven thee.
> ⁶ But there was certain of the scribes sitting there, and reasoning in their hearts,
> ⁷ Why doth this man thus speak blasphemies? who can forgive sins but God only?
> ⁸ And immediately when Jesus perceived in his spirit that they so reasoned within themselves, he said unto them, Why reason ye these

> *things in your hearts?*
> *⁹ Whether is it easier to say to the sick of the palsy, Thy sins be forgiven thee; or to say, Arise, and take up thy bed, and walk?*
> *¹⁰ But that ye may know that the Son of man hath power on earth to forgive sins, (he saith to the sick of the palsy,)*
> *¹¹ I say unto thee, Arise, and take up thy bed, and go thy way into thine house.*
> *¹² And immediately he arose, took up the bed, and went forth before them all; insomuch that they were all amazed, and glorified God, saying, We never saw it on this fashion.*
>
> Mark 2:3-12

The power of God you manifest cannot exceed your knowledge of Him. The people said, who can forgive sins but God? This situation was an opportunity for Jesus to demonstrate that He had power on earth to forgive sins. This is a very fascinating story that rocks the boat of modern theology. Can one man forgive the sins of another man? Did Jesus forgive the sins of this man as God or did He forgive the sin as man? Someone may say, but Jesus was not man. Really? Which part of this story then was God and which one was man? If He forgave as God, then we would need to determine which things Jesus did as God and which ones He did as man to determine what we can aspire to. If He forgave as man, this would imply that one man operating under the power of the Holy Spirit can forgive the sins of another man thereby demonstrating the God-like characteristic.

> *²¹ Then said Jesus to them again, Peace be unto you: as my Father hath sent me, even so send I you.*
> *²² And when he had said this, he breathed on them, and saith unto them, Receive ye the Holy Ghost:*
> *²³ Whose soever sins ye remit, they are remitted unto them; and whose soever sins ye retain, they are retained.*
>
> John 20:21-24

Jesus was travelling in a boat with His disciples when a

storm arose and the man with God-like characteristics went into action.

> ²³ And when he was entered into a ship, his disciples followed him.
> ²⁴ And, behold, there arose a great tempest in the sea, insomuch that the ship was covered with the waves: but he was asleep.
> ²⁵ And his disciples came to him, and awoke him, saying, Lord, save us: we perish.
> ²⁶ And he saith unto them, Why are ye fearful, O ye of little faith? Then he arose, and rebuked the winds and the sea; and there was a great calm.
> ²⁷ But the men marvelled, saying, What manner of man is this, that even the winds and the sea obey him!
>
> Matthew 8:23-27

Oh that we would begin to walk in this authority given to us. If we claim to be sons of God, we must exhibit the characteristics of God both in the fruits of our character and in the power of the kingdom. Remember, the kingdom of God is not in word only but also in power. A fish does not need to *learn* to swim. By nature, they swim. When we get born-again, we have the nature of God. We only need to manifest what is in us like Jesus manifested his glory in Canaan.

> ¹¹ This beginning of miracles did Jesus in Cana of Galilee, and manifested forth his glory; and his disciples believed on him.
>
> John 2:11

Glory be to God. His mercy endures forever and His love is from everlasting to everlasting. We need to start walking in the reality of the resurrection of Christ. We have been darkened in our understanding for too long, the time to be liberated is now.

> ¹⁷ This I say therefore, and testify in the Lord, that ye henceforth walk not as other Gentiles walk, in the vanity of their mind,

> *¹⁸ Having the understanding darkened, BEING ALIENATED from the life of God THROUGH THE IGNORANCE that is in them, because of the blindness of their heart:*
>
> Ephesians 4:17-18

It is ignorance, that is, the absence of relevant knowledge that cause believers to be alienated from the life of God which in turn results in living a defeated life.

As the prophet Ezekiel prophesied to the dry bones, I speak to every dry area in your life that you desire fruitfulness and I command it to receive the breath of life now, in Jesus name. I command every dead dream, every dead vision, every dead idea to come alive now and live to become an exceeding great army in the land, in Jesus name.

Paul admonishes us to come boldly before the throne of grace that we may obtain mercy. (*Heb 4:13*). The veil of the temple has been torn in two and God, our Father has made us able ministers of the New Testament. We now have an open relationship with God. *(2 Corinthians 3:6-18)*

Riches and Wealth

One of the by products of knowledge is Riches and wealth. You can have riches and wealth and not possess wisdom and knowledge, but you cannot have wisdom and knowledge and not have riches and wealth. You may ask how can that be, see what Elihu had to say to Job's friends;

> *⁶ And Elihu the son of Barachel the Buzite answered and said, I am young, and ye are very old; wherefore I was afraid, and durst not shew you mine opinion.*
> *⁷ I said, Days should speak, and multitude of years should teach wisdom.*
> *⁸ But there is a spirit in man: and the inspiration of the Almighty giveth them understanding.*

The Rewards of Knowledge

> ⁹ GREAT MEN ARE NOT ALWAYS WISE: NEITHER DO THE AGED UNDERSTAND JUDGMENT.
> ¹⁰ Therefore I said, Hearken to me; I also will shew mine opinion.
> ¹¹ Behold, I waited for your words; I gave ear to your reasons, whilst ye searched out what to say.
> ¹² Yea, I attended unto you, and, behold, there was none of you that convinced Job, or that answered his words:
>
> Job 32:6-12

Let us see the story of a man who went after wisdom and knowledge and what he got.

> ⁸ And Solomon said unto God, Thou hast shewed great mercy unto David my father, and hast made me to reign in his stead.
> ⁹ Now, O LORD God, let thy promise unto David my father be established: for thou hast made me king over a people like the dust of the earth in multitude.
> ¹⁰ Give me now wisdom and knowledge, that I may go out and come in before this people: for who can judge this thy people, that is so great?
> ¹¹ AND GOD SAID TO SOLOMON, BECAUSE THIS WAS IN THINE HEART, AND THOU HAST NOT ASKED RICHES, WEALTH, OR HONOUR, NOR THE LIFE OF THINE ENEMIES, NEITHER YET HAST ASKED LONG LIFE; BUT HAST ASKED WISDOM AND KNOWLEDGE FOR THYSELF, that thou mayest judge my people, over whom I have made thee king:
> ¹² WISDOM AND KNOWLEDGE IS GRANTED UNTO THEE; AND I WILL GIVE THEE RICHES, AND WEALTH, AND HONOUR, such as none of the kings have had that have been before thee, neither shall there any after thee have the like.
>
> 2 Chronicles 1:8-12

The manifestation of the church is truly a glorious one and we are in those last days now. This path to a great destiny has already been laid bare before us. We need to observe this and not let it depart from our mouth and our hearts that we may observe to do likewise.

In times of instability, it is through wisdom and knowledge that we are established.

> ⁶ And wisdom and knowledge shall be the stability of thy times, and strength of salvation: the fear of the LORD is his treasure.
>
> *Isaiah 33:6*

Freedom

Freedom is an interesting concept. I believe a lot of people do not reach their full potential in life because of their fear of one negative thing or the other happening but knowledge shows the exit door through the strongholds of life. Freedom, for me, means *"free to dominate"* or *"free to exercise dominion"* or better still *"right to be who the Word of God say you are"*.

> ³² And ye shall know the truth, and the truth shall make you free.
>
> *John 8:32*

The knowledge of the truth required for freedom here is similar to the one referred to in *Daniel 1:17*. It refers to absolute awareness of the truth with the ability to speak it with understanding. It describes the place where you get to and you can rightly divide the Word of Truth. It is having a multifaceted understanding of the same topic.

> ¹⁵ Study to shew thyself approved unto God, a workman that needeth not to be ashamed, rightly dividing the word of truth.
>
> *2 Timothy 2:15*

It is the understanding you get not only from hearing, reading or studying the word. It includes the knowledge that gets imparted when you have experienced the truth. Many people know things that they have never experienced but what you have experienced, you are convinced of.

> ¹ That which was from the beginning, which we have heard, which we have seen with our eyes, which we have looked upon, and our hands have handled, of the Word of life;

² *(For the life was manifested, and we have seen it, and bear witness, and shew unto you that eternal life, which was with the Father, and was manifested unto us;)*
³ *That which we have seen and heard declare we unto you, that ye also may have fellowship with us: and truly our fellowship is with the Father, and with his Son Jesus Christ.*
⁴ *And these things write we unto you, that your joy may be full.*

1 John 1:1-4

Many times in our quest for freedom and liberty, we apply the same principles of the world which seems right but leads to bondage. There is a process of continuing in the word of God until we begin to experience its realities.

²¹ *Wherefore lay apart all filthiness and superfluity of naughtiness, and receive with meekness the engrafted word, which is able to save your souls.*
²² *But be ye doers of the word, and not hearers only, deceiving your own selves.*
²³ *For if any be a hearer of the word, and not a doer, he is like unto a man beholding his natural face in a glass:*
²⁴ *For he beholdeth himself, and goeth his way, and straightway forgetteth what manner of man he was.*
²⁵ *But whoso looketh into the perfect law of liberty, and continueth therein, he being not a forgetful hearer, but a doer of the work, this man shall be blessed in his deed.*

James 1:21-25

Freedom through knowledge only comes when the knowledge is acted upon. Without being a *doer* of knowledge, we will never experience its rewards. I pray that as you continue in your study on knowledge, you start to brace yourself for change.

Chapter Key Points

Just knowing makes you a reference point but getting results with knowledge makes you an achiever.

Everyone that walks and lives under the influence of this breath exhibits "God-like" characteristics

The area in which you experience weakness is usually the area in which the Word of God has not become a reality in your life

Freedom, for me, means "*free to dominate*" or "*free to exercise dominion*" or better still "*right to be who the Word of God say you are*".

6

Knowledge for Exploits

God wants His chosen people to walk in this dimension of knowledge and give Him pleasure. Never before has this depth of knowledge with its practical application been more required in the Church of our Lord and Saviour Jesus Christ.

This is our season for shinning. The light is shinning in the midst of darkness. From the midst of the dry places comes the spring of life. The abundance of life is manifested. The time is here. Now our Faith is.

Let us look at examples of this supernatural ability of God at work in people who had a relationship with Him. There is nothing manifested by the Spirit in the individuals we will be looking at here that is not available to us in much greater dimensions now. Our inheritance in Christ gives us access to the Holy of Holies. If the blessing of Abraham, being physically dead for generations, is available to us today through Christ, the grace on anyone in the scriptures and any believer now living is available to you by believing and asking in faith. Remember, Joshua was full of the spirit of wisdom because Moses had laid hands on him (*Deuteronomy 34:9*). Again God took of the spirit that was on Moses and transferred it to seventy elders of Israel.

> [16] *And the LORD said unto Moses, Gather unto me seventy men of the elders of Israel, whom thou knowest to be the elders of the people, and officers over them; and bring them unto the tabernacle of the congregation, that they may stand there with thee.*
> [17] *And I will come down and talk with thee there:* **AND I WILL TAKE OF THE SPIRIT WHICH IS UPON THEE, AND WILL PUT IT UPON THEM**; *and they shall bear the burden of the people with thee, that thou bear it not thyself alone.*
>
> Numbers 11:16-17

When I read this story of Moses, I wondered why God took of the spirit that was on Moses. Why did God not give them their own? Was He not the source of it all? I have found that one of the easiest ways to get spiritual messages across to people is by using those around them. Jesus talked about a man's enemy being those of this own household. What did He mean? Those closest to you are either your greatest supporters or your greatest hindrances. If there is a grace you desire, be in close proximity with those that have it or in close proximity with their work. You or anything that comes out of you is a channel for the transference of your grace to another whether they know you or not.

The New Testament also shows us a similar pattern of this gift of God passing from one person to another. In this case, from Apostle Paul to Timothy.

> [6] *Wherefore I put thee in remembrance that thou stir up the gift of God, which is in thee by the putting on of my hands.*
>
> 2 Timothy 1:6

How did the gift get into Timothy? By the laying on of the

hands of Paul. This does not mean that the only way for the spirit to transfer from one man to another is through the laying on of hands but the laying on of hands is a scriptural method. *Hebrews 6:1-2* talks about the doctrine of laying on of hands. It is the same God who was mighty in them that is working in us and it is the same Holy Spirit operating in us. Let faith arise in you as you embrace these truths. This Holy Spirit that is in our hearts delivers to us a higher level of access to the things of God. What the patriarchs of faith in *Hebrews 11* only saw afar off and never handled we can handle. Paul speaking about these ones in the book of Hebrews had this to say.

> *39 AND THESE ALL, HAVING OBTAINED A GOOD REPORT THROUGH FAITH, RECEIVED NOT THE PROMISE:*
> *40 God having provided some better thing for us, that they without us should not be made perfect.*
>
> *Hebrews 11:39-40*

What! They had a good report through faith but not the promise? What is the promise referred to here? The promise was the Word of God becoming flesh and living on the earth. The promise is God making His tabernacle with man. In the Old Testament, God visited man but in the New Testament, God lives in man. What does God living in you mean? It means when you see a man full of the Spirit of God, you are seeing God manifesting in the flesh.

> *14 AND THE WORD WAS MADE FLESH, AND DWELT AMONG US, (and we beheld his glory, the glory as of the only begotten of the Father,) full of grace and truth.*
>
> *John 1:14*

How do we know this? See what Jesus said concerning Abraham.

> *56 Your father Abraham rejoiced to see my day: and he saw it, and*

was glad.

John 8:56

Abraham saw the day of Jesus and was glad. A seeing that made him become the father of faith. How can a man living hundreds of years before Christ rejoice in the day of Christ and be glad? Abraham saw what it would be like after Christ had died and started rejoicing. Wow! What great faith. Can you picture yourself operating in the knowledge we are talking about here? See it. Rejoice in it. Be glad. Give God praise and you will see the salvation of God.

Believe in Me, Believe in Me and you will see exploits beyond your imagination says the Lord.

The hope that Abraham had kept him trusting God and holding on to His Word. These patriarchs only saw this blessed day as Moses saw the promised land but they never experienced it. I pray God gives you understanding of this truth that I am about to bring to you. If through belief and faith in the day of Christ *{generations in the future}* that these patriarchs saw in their mind, they were able to do the great exploits that stir up faith in our spirits today. How great is the access given to us in our time. What a priviledge to be alive in the future they saw.

> *¹ That which was from the beginning, which we have heard, which we have seen with our eyes, which we have looked upon, and our hands have handled, of the Word of life;*
> *² (For the life was manifested, and we have seen it, and bear witness, and shew unto you that eternal life, which was with the Father, and was manifested unto us;)*
> *³ That which we have seen and heard declare we unto you, that ye also may have fellowship with us: and truly our fellowship is with the Father, and with his Son Jesus Christ.*
> *⁴ And these things write we unto you, that your joy may be full.*
>
> *1 John 1:1-4*

What a glorious revelation. The life was manifested and we have seen it. In our time, in our season, we have become the temple of this Life. We are living in the dispensation that Abraham saw. How can we display less hope than he did? The life that makes God God is now resident in us.

> *19 What? know ye not that your body is the temple of the Holy Ghost which is in you, which ye have of God, and ye are not your own?*
> *20 For ye are bought with a price: therefore glorify God in your body, and in your spirit, which are God's.*
>
> 1 Corinthians 6:19-20

Hallelujah! As I write, I can feel the life pulsating in my being. Glory to God, we can talk with language that before now was not conceivable. The Almighty God, the creator of the heavens and the earth, the Possessor of eternity, the One without beginning of days, neither end of life gave his ONLY son for you and I. He bought us with a price. God understands the concept of value is not a loss making God. If in the estimation of God, the right price for us was His only Son. Then at a minimum, our value to God should be equal to the value of the Son He gave in order for Him not to make a loss.

> *17... because as he is, so are we in this world.*
>
> 1 John 4:17

Imagine the level of reality of God and this knowledge that Moses the great prophet of Israel walked in, yet this is below the level the Believer with the indwelling Spirit operates in. Anything below what was manifested in Moses is the ministration of death because this ministration of Moses faded with time.

> *7 But if the ministration of death, written and engraven in stones, was glorious, so that the children of Israel could not stedfastly behold the face of Moses for the glory of his countenance; which glory was to be*

done away:

⁸ How shall not the ministration of the spirit be rather glorious?

⁹ For if the ministration of condemnation be glory, much more doth the ministration of righteousness exceed in glory.

¹⁰ For even that which was made glorious had no glory in this respect, by reason of the glory that excelleth.

¹¹ For if that which is done away was glorious, much more that which remaineth is glorious.

¹² Seeing then that we have such hope, we use great plainness of speech:

¹³ And not as Moses, which put a veil over his face, that the children of Israel could not stedfastly look to the end of that which is abolished:

¹⁴ But their minds were blinded: for until this day remaineth the same vail untaken away in the reading of the old testament; which vail is done away in Christ.

¹⁵ But even unto this day, when Moses is read, the vail is upon their heart.

¹⁶ Nevertheless when it shall turn to the Lord, the vail shall be taken away.

¹⁷ Now the Lord is that Spirit: and where the Spirit of the Lord is, there is liberty.

¹⁸ But we all, with open face beholding as in a glass the glory of the Lord, are changed into the same image from glory to glory, even as by the Spirit of the Lord.

2 Corinthians 3:7-18

To believe you are less than God says you are in His Word is to cut short your destiny. I encourage you to step out in faith and do not abort the life of God that is flowing in you.

Abortion is generally considered to be the termination of the life of an unborn child. But if God truly is the author of life, which He is, would that not imply that even before a sperm fertilizes an egg, a purpose for that life would have been orchestrated in heaven, and a carrier created on earth for the delivery of that life's purpose?

The Prophet Jeremiah recounts the word of the Lord to him saying;

> ⁵ *Before I formed thee in the belly I knew thee; and before thou camest forth out of the womb I sanctified thee, and I ordained thee a prophet unto the nations.*
>
> Jeremiah 1:5

Apostle Paul also says;

> ¹⁵ *But when it pleased God, who separated me from my mother's womb, and called me by his grace,*
> ¹⁶ *To reveal his Son in me, that I might preach him among the heathen; immediately I conferred not with flesh and blood:*
>
> Galatians 1:15-16

From the life of these prophets of God, we can see that Life does not happen by chance but when the breath of life from God enters someone. For example, man did not become a living soul until the life of God entered him (*Genesis 2:7*). After this life entered Adam, he had the ability to be like God. He could dream like God. Abortion then is the taking away of life from a dream. I have concluded that abortion is considered an option when the possibility of a bright future for both the carrier (*man*) and the carried (*the dream*) cannot be found in the mind of the carrier. If there were no limitations in the mind of the carrier, if all things were possible to the carrier, if anything that was imagined by the carrier could be a possibility, would abortion still be an option? If the depth of life that I am talking about here is possible, what excuses do you have for not pursing this dimension of the life of God. Shortly, we will see real stories of demonstrations of this life.

What would have happened if the Wright brothers who gave us aeroplanes had given up on the dream; if Thomas Edison, one of the most prolific inventors this world has known had aborted the dreams that led to his inventions; if Bill Gates had given up on the Microsoft dream? Can you imagine if Joseph's brothers had killed Joseph, the carrier of the dream that would preserve them, the deliverer of their future (*Genesis 37:18-20*); If David had listened to Eliab, he would never have fought Goliath (*1 Samuel 17:23-30*); if Abraham had settled for Ishmael, he would never have had Isaac (*Genesis 17:16-19*); if Joshua and Caleb had listened to the other ten spies, they would never have entered the Promised Land (*Numbers 13:26-33*); if Mary, the mother of Jesus had decided to terminate that pregnancy where would be salvation; if Jesus had listened to Peter, he would never have gone to the Cross (*Matthew 16:21-23*); if Peter had listened to the other Jews, the Gentiles would never have received the Holy Spirit (*Acts 11:1-2*). Are you beginning to see the bigger picture?

Now imagine that like Mary who carried the pregnancy of Jesus, you carry ideas and dreams that flood your mind continuously. These ideas have made a strong impression on your heart; it's even been with you since you were young. As you are reading this now, your memory is kicking into action. You remember those dreams and they probably bring a smile to your face. No matter what you do, the ideas keep coming and you can't get them out of your mind. Like Joseph, you may even have started talking about your dream and suddenly from the least expected sources (*family & friends*) you start to hear the reasons why it cannot be done. You become a laughing stock for having an idea that seems to be out of season (*Consider Noah & Abraham*). Rejection comes from all sources because the very mention of these ideas is becoming an offence to some. Jesus said, *"blessed is he who is not offended in me"*. People simply do not understand why you cannot be normal. Considering that once you get to tomorrow, today's normal is considered as being backward and stuck in the past, have you ever wondered, what exactly does it means to be normal? After all, Joseph's brothers were normal as were all David's brothers. At least, so they thought.

I cannot help but think that many people may have aborted those dreams God put in their heart to deliver a resting place in their future, yet they have aborted it. God is giving you another chance through the knowledge I am sharing here.

Remember those divine relationships God has given you that are not being nurtured and the God-allowed circumstances for which shortcuts are being sought may be there to trigger your God-given dream which ultimately will be the answer for generations yet unborn. You may think that your dream is too far-fetched to become a reality. Well, you are in good company. Abraham thought the same, so did Mary the mother of Jesus (*Luke 1:34*) and Mary the sister of Lazarus (*John 11:32*). Not left out are the servants that told the centurion not to trouble the Master any further (*Mark 8:49*), or the mourners that stood outside the house of the young damsel (*Mark 8:53*).

Now, the Bible declares that the day cometh, that the dead in the grave will hear the voice of the son of man and live. That day is now. In the name of Jesus Christ, I command every dead dream to come to life. As Lazarus heard the voice of Jesus and responded, so every dream of your desire hears my voice and comes to life. By the power in the name of Jesus, every mountain before you is made plain. Arise, dust yourself, all things are ready.

Remember, nothing is impossible to him that believes. Nothing is impossible to him who actively trusts in the power of the spoken Word of God to effect change. How dark the future will be if your dream does not become a reality.

Chapter Key Points

If the blessing of Abraham, being physically dead for generations, is available to us today through Christ, the grace on anyone in the scriptures and any believer now living is available to you by believing and asking in faith

What does God living in you mean? It means when you see a man full of the Spirit of God, you are seeing God manifesting in the flesh

We are living in the dispensation that Abraham saw. How can we display less hope than he did?

To believe you are less than God says you are in His word is to cut short your destiny

7

Demonstrations of Knowledge

With the truth on knowledge for exploits in mind, I also use plainness of speech as we look at the different dimensions of this life available to us now. Let the veils come off in the name of Jesus, receive grace for this unfolding Word which is able to save your souls.

Let us look at some real life people who have served as examples for us and whose footsteps we can follow. These are normal people who through the application of this same knowledge we are talking about have been able to distinguish themselves.

The Intelligence of Adam

What a force that was as work in Adam before the fall.

> [19] *And out of the ground the LORD God formed every beast of the field, and every fowl of the air; and brought them unto Adam to see what he would call them:* **AND WHATSOEVER ADAM CALLED EVERY LIVING CREATURE, THAT WAS THE NAME THEREOF.**

²⁰ And Adam gave names to all cattle, and to the fowl of the air, and to every beast of the field; but for Adam there was not found an help meet for him.

Genesis 2:19-20

I do not know how long it took for Adam to come up with all these names but he had not attended any school or institution on memory development, creative thinking or visualisation. He had just been created and put in the garden to dress it and keep it and God had only just formed these beasts of the field and fowls of the air before bringing them to Adam. As Adam was only meeting them for the first time, I imagine that Adam must have examined each one of these creatures and given them names that were appropriate to their characteristics without consulting any manuals. The potency of the life that was in him ensured perfect understanding and memory to ensure that the names were not conflicting.

By the power of the Holy Spirit and in the name of Jesus that lives forever more, I command this same order of intelligence to start to manifest in you from this day forward. Shine in your time.

We are not told anywhere that God renamed any of these cattle, birds or beasts. I am sure God was looking over what Adam was doing and was pleased with it. You may say, well, that was before the fall, things do not quite work that way. Jesus, our perfect example also demonstrated extraordinary mental capacity at the age of twelve.

⁴⁶ And it came to pass, that after three days they found him in the temple, sitting in the midst of the doctors, both hearing them, and asking them questions.
⁴⁷ And all that heard him were astonished at his understanding and answers.

Luke 2:46-47

The Amplified Bible makes this verse come alive.

⁴⁶ After three days they found Him [came upon Him] in the [court of the] temple, sitting among the teachers, listening to them and asking them questions.
⁴⁷ And all who heard Him were astonished and overwhelmed with bewildered wonder at His intelligence and understanding and His replies.

Luke 2:46-47 (AMP)

With a little peek into the Greek, we discover that Jesus' understanding and answers outwitted these doctors of the law almost to the point of insanity making them act like they were under the influence of a controlling spirit. This state is probably what Paul referred to in his letter to the Ephesian Church when he warned them not be drunk with wine, but be filled with the Spirit. (*Ephesians 5:18*). Sometimes the unveiling of the word of God in your heart makes you act in a not too dignified way, forgetting your environment and with your focus totally on God.

Almost every diligent student of the Bible has one particular Bible. The *Dake's Annotated Referencce Bible*. While a lot of Bible students use this reference Bible, not many know the story of the Author, Finis Jennings Dake (*1902-1987*).

[1]It is said that not only did Dake's know the true meaning of almost every word in the Bible, he also knew the opinions of different Bible scholars on subjects. In a challenge from a preacher, Dake's quoted the entire New Testament from Matthew to Revelation giving the exact number of each verse and chapter changes without opening a Bible. Dake's is quoted as being aware of this supernatural ability following the experience of the baptism of the Holy Spirit. It was not an ability he possessed prior to this experience.

---

1 Pg 67-72, Pioneers of Faith, Lester Sumrall

In a conference in June 2010 in London, Rev George Adegboye of the Rhema Chapel International Ministries in a message on faith quoted over one hundred scriptures almost verbatim without looking at the Bible during a teaching session that lasted over 60 minutes. He also credits this ability to a supernatural grace from God.

These two men, like the Hebrew boys still gave themselves to the development of their gifts through diligent study and practical steps. It is reported that Dakes spent over 10,000 hours on his work, overnight for many days on several occasions. Adegboye is said to have read the Bible over 200 times. Every grace obtained from God requires practical steps to be engaged if we are to grow in them.

The Might of Abraham

Imagine a man having his own private army with strength and strategies powerful enough to overcome a confederation of kings.

> *[1] And it came to pass in the days of Amraphel king of Shinar, Arioch king of Ellasar, Chedorlaomer king of Elam, and Tidal king of nations;*
> *[2] That these made war with Bera king of Sodom, and with Birsha king of Gomorrah, Shinab king of Admah, and Shemeber king of Zeboiim, and the king of Bela, which is Zoar.*
> *[3] All these were joined together in the vale of Siddim, which is the salt sea.*
> *[4] Twelve years they served Chedorlaomer, and in the thirteenth year they rebelled.*
> *[5] And in the fourteenth year came Chedorlaomer, and the kings that were with him, and smote the Rephaims in Ashteroth Karnaim, and the Zuzims in Ham, and the Emins in Shaveh Kiriathaim,*
> *[6] And the Horites in their mount Seir, unto Elparan, which is by the wilderness.*
> *[7] And they returned, and came to Enmishpat, which is Kadesh, and smote all the country of the Amalekites, and also the Amorites, that*

dwelt in Hazezontamar.
⁸ And there went out the king of Sodom, and the king of Gomorrah, and the king of Admah, and the king of Zeboiim, and the king of Bela (the same is Zoar;) and they joined battle with them in the vale of Siddim;
⁹ With Chedorlaomer the king of Elam, and with Tidal king of nations, and Amraphel king of Shinar, and Arioch king of Ellasar; four kings with five.
¹⁰ And the vale of Siddim was full of slimepits; and the kings of Sodom and Gomorrah fled, and fell there; and they that remained fled to the mountain.
¹¹ And they took all the goods of Sodom and Gomorrah, and all their victuals, and went their way.
¹² And they took Lot, Abram's brother's son, who dwelt in Sodom, and his goods, and departed.
¹³ And there came one that had escaped, and told Abram the Hebrew; for he dwelt in the plain of Mamre the Amorite, brother of Eshcol, and brother of Aner: and these were confederate with Abram.
¹⁴ And when Abram heard that his brother was taken captive, he armed his trained servants, born in his own house, three hundred and eighteen, and pursued them unto Dan.
¹⁵ And he divided himself against them, he and his servants, by night, and smote them, and pursued them unto Hobah, which is on the left hand of Damascus.
¹⁶ And he brought back all the goods, and also brought again his brother Lot, and his goods, and the women also, and the people.

Genesis 14:1-16

In case you do not appreciate this scenario, let me paint a picture for you. This is like a private man rising up in a country and saying he will take on United Nations forces because they captured his cousin as a prisoner of war. This man Abraham had three hundred and eighteen servants, born and trained in his own house and he also had the necessary arms to go to war with.

You may say but that was in those days, surely it is illegal for people to store arms and have private armies in these days. You may be right but the real question is this. Have you invested in the development of people around you to the degree that they are willing to go to war with you in the day of battle? Might goes beyond the exhibition of physical strength. It is the ability to push an agenda through without inhibition.

The wars of this time are fought based on information. The army that is able to identify the command centre and commanders of the opponent is more likely to win a war than the army that does not have this knowledge. Intelligence is a key component of might. Without intelligence, might has no direction and might without direction is useless. If Abraham did not know where his cousin had been taken, there is no way he would have been able to recover that which was stolen.

A lot of times because we do not talk about the might of God, we do not see manifestations along this line. We only focus on the manifestations talked about in the New Testament. (*1 Corinthians 12:9*) and yet men like Elijah, Samson and David's mighty men operated in the spirit of might (*Isaiah 11:1-2*)

> [44] *And it came to pass at the seventh time, that he said, Behold, there ariseth a little cloud out of the sea, like a man's hand. And he said, Go up, say unto Ahab, Prepare thy chariot, and get thee down that the rain stop thee not.*
> [45] *And it came to pass in the mean while, that the heaven was black with clouds and wind, and there was a great rain. And Ahab rode, and went to Jezreel.*
> [46] *And the hand of the LORD was on Elijah; and he girded up his loins, and ran before Ahab to the entrance of Jezreel.*
>
> 1 Kings 18:44-46

How did Elijah outrun a man on a chariot pulled by horses? By the hand of the Lord and the spirit of might. How about Samson and David who both killed lions with a little more than bare hands. David's mighty men remain a great inspiration.

> ⁸ These be the names of the mighty men whom David had: The Tachmonite that sat in the seat, chief among the captains; the same was Adino the Eznite: he lift up his spear against eight hundred, whom he slew at one time.
> ⁹ And after him was Eleazar the son of Dodo the Ahohite, one of the three mighty men with David, when they defied the Philistines that were there gathered together to battle, and the men of Israel were gone away:
> ¹⁰ He arose, and smote the Philistines until his hand was weary, and his hand clave unto the sword: and the LORD wrought a great victory that day; and the people returned after him only to spoil.
> ¹¹ And after him was Shammah the son of Agee the Hararite. And the Philistines were gathered together into a troop, where was a piece of ground full of lentiles: and the people fled from the Philistines.
> ¹² But he stood in the midst of the ground, and defended it, and slew the Philistines: and the LORD wrought a great victory.
> ¹³ And three of the thirty chief went down, and came to David in the harvest time unto the cave of Adullam: and the troop of the Philistines pitched in the valley of Rephaim.
> ¹⁴ And David was then in an hold, and the garrison of the Philistines was then in Bethlehem.
> ¹⁵ And David longed, and said, Oh that one would give me drink of the water of the well of Bethlehem, which is by the gate!
> ¹⁶ And the three mighty men brake through the host of the Philistines, and drew water out of the well of Bethlehem, that was by the gate, and took it, and brought it to David: nevertheless he would not drink thereof, but poured it out unto the LORD.
> ¹⁷ And he said, Be it far from me, O LORD, that I should do this: is not this the blood of the men that went in jeopardy of their lives? therefore he would not drink it. These things did these three mighty men.
> ¹⁸ And Abishai, the brother of Joab, the son of Zeruiah, was chief among three. And he lifted up his spear against three hundred, and slew them, and had the name among three.
> ¹⁹ Was he not most honourable of three? therefore he was their captain: howbeit he attained not unto the first three.
> ²⁰ And Benaiah the son of Jehoiada, the son of a valiant man, of Kabzeel, who had done many acts, he slew two lionlike men of Moab:

> he went down also and slew a lion in the midst of a pit in time of snow: ²¹ And he slew an Egyptian, a goodly man: and the Egyptian had a spear in his hand; but he went down to him with a staff, and plucked the spear out of the Egyptian's hand, and slew him with his own spear.
>
> 2 Samuel 23: 8-21

How do you slay eight hundred men with a spear at one time (*2 Samuel 23:8*)? I tried to imagine this. Was he circled by a group of enemy soldiers while he held a long spear? I can only imagine that from where he was, he threw the spear with such force that it went right through eight hundred people before stopping. This could only have been the spirit of might in operation.

Now this story of David and his great men present significant insight into relationship building. Remember David himself was a man of might.

> ³³ And Saul said to David, Thou art not able to go against this Philistine to fight with him: for thou art but a youth, and he a man of war from his youth.
> ³⁴ And David said unto Saul, Thy servant kept his father's sheep, and there came a lion, and a bear, and took a lamb out of the flock:
> ³⁵ And I went out after him, and smote him, and delivered it out of his mouth: and when he arose against me, I caught him by his beard, and smote him, and slew him.
> ³⁶ Thy servant slew both the lion and the bear: and this uncircumcised Philistine shall be as one of them, seeing he hath defied the armies of the living God.
> ³⁷ David said moreover, The LORD that delivered me out of the paw of the lion, and out of the paw of the bear, he will deliver me out of the hand of this Philistine. And Saul said unto David, Go, and the LORD be with thee.
>
> 1 Samuel 17:33-37

What is my point on this? David attracted men who were like himself or men he could build to be like himself. Even Jesus attracted people who would be like Him. I strongly believe that a lot of times we attract as friends people who share the same convictions in our strengths, likes and beliefs. Many times, these people have the same weakness as we do. Unless we make conscious decisions around these weak areas, these weakness remain unchecked and could become major strongholds and doors through which the enemy can attack us. Any area of weakness just indicates an area you which you have not expended sufficient developmental energy.

A lot of what we call generational curses are really only areas where our parents lacked knowledge and therefore could not provide us with the wisdom and knowledge to overcome in those areas. If we do not acquire knowledge in these areas to pass to our children and our children do not acquire this knowledge external to the home, they will exhibit the same deficiency. So, before you jump on the generational curse bandwagon, check your ignorance.

While in these present day we do not fight against flesh and blood as described in these examples, There are enough signs to show us that the spirit of might is still the same today. Have you considered all those bursts of energy that make you complete tasks in a fraction of the time, that makes you work extended periods on the things of God yet still feeling fresh as when you started, are all manifestations of the spirit of might. How about the supernatural energy that comes upon you in the place of prayer and causes you to pray through forces of darkness?

May the God of Abraham and the God of Elisha the prophet strengthen you with might for every economic battle that faces you. Let angelic assistance follow you in the name of Jesus. Go and recover all. There shall be no more loss in your business. You expand from this day forward. Supernatural information in measures unthinkable is available to you in all your dealings in the name of Jesus.

Might by the Holy Spirit brought deliverance to Israel. This same Spirit is at work in you and as you connect with the divine associations God has orchestrated for you, may you experience the supernatural levels of deliverance in Jesus name.

During this crucifixion of Jesus, remember his response to the king.

> ^{47} And while he yet spake, lo, Judas, one of the twelve, came, and with him a great multitude with swords and staves, from the chief priests and elders of the people.
> ^{48} Now he that betrayed him gave them a sign, saying, Whomsoever I shall kiss, that same is he: hold him fast.
> ^{49} And forthwith he came to Jesus, and said, Hail, master; and kissed him.
> ^{50} And Jesus said unto him, Friend, wherefore art thou come? Then came they, and laid hands on Jesus and took him.
> ^{51} And, behold, one of them which were with Jesus stretched out his hand, and drew his sword, and struck a servant of the high priest's, and smote off his ear.
> ^{52} Then said Jesus unto him, Put up again thy sword into his place: for all they that take the sword shall perish with the sword.
> ^{53} **THINKEST THOU THAT I CANNOT NOW PRAY TO MY FATHER, AND HE SHALL PRESENTLY GIVE ME MORE THAN TWELVE LEGIONS OF ANGELS?**
> ^{54}But how then shall the scriptures be fulfilled, that thus it must be?
>
> *Matthew 26:47-54*

Jesus signified that the decision not to use the supernatural might available to Him was a conscious decision and not a lack of might. One final point here. The fact that you have access to supernatural might does not mean it should be used in every instance. Understanding the will of God in specific situations should override everything.

The Innovation of Jacob

Innovation is going to be one of the vehicles God will use to empower the Church in these last days. Once again, this innovation is based on our ability to know what to do when it appears all we currently know is no longer delivering the results we expect. Innovation determines how we negotiate deals. I remember when computer software was relatively new, software was just gaining momentum and the pricing model was one called a perpetual licence. Once you bought the software, you owned it and there were no more fees due to the software manufacturer. This licencing model has now innovated over the years. A lot of software providers now have a subscription model which provides income on an agreed timetable. I am sure a number of computer companies are still in existence today because they switched to this new model.

The spirit of innovation allows us to create scenarios in the life that were before unthinkable. Without this knowledge at work in us, we will turn down deals that judging by the natural mind seem impossible to execute on. Most breakthrough deals that inspire us are deals that were driven by chance. What is chance but an opportunity for which you were prepared. When preparation meets chance, elevation is inevitable.

There was something Jacob knew that enabled him to transfer the wealth of Laban to himself.

> [27] And Laban said unto him, I pray thee, if I have found favour in thine eyes, tarry: for I have learned by experience that the LORD hath blessed me for thy sake.
> [28] And he said, Appoint me thy wages, and I will give it.
> [29] And he said unto him, Thou knowest how I have served thee, and how thy cattle was with me.
> [30] For it was little which thou hadst before I came, and it is now

increased unto a multitude; and the LORD hath blessed thee since my coming: and now when shall I provide for mine own house also? ³¹ And he said, What shall I give thee? And Jacob said, Thou shalt not give me any thing: if thou wilt do this thing for me, I will again feed and keep thy flock.

³² I will pass through all thy flock to day, removing from thence all the speckled and spotted cattle, and all the brown cattle among the sheep, and the spotted and speckled among the goats: and of such shall be my hire.

³³ So shall my righteousness answer for me in time to come, when it shall come for my hire before thy face: every one that is not speckled and spotted among the goats, and brown among the sheep, that shall be counted stolen with me.

³⁴ And Laban said, Behold, I would it might be according to thy word.

³⁵ And he removed that day the he goats that were ringstraked and spotted, and all the she goats that were speckled and spotted, and every one that had some white in it, and all the brown among the sheep, and gave them into the hand of his sons.

³⁶ And he set three days' journey betwixt himself and Jacob: and Jacob fed the rest of Laban's flocks.

³⁷ And Jacob took him rods of green poplar, and of the hazel and chesnut tree; and pilled white strakes in them, and made the white appear which was in the rods.

³⁸ And he set the rods which he had pilled before the flocks in the gutters in the watering troughs when the flocks came to drink, that they should conceive when they came to drink.

³⁹ And the flocks conceived before the rods, and brought forth cattle ringstraked, speckled, and spotted.

⁴⁰ And Jacob did separate the lambs, and set the faces of the flocks toward the ringstraked, and all the brown in the flock of Laban; and he put his own flocks by themselves, and put them not unto Laban's cattle.

⁴¹ And it came to pass, whensoever the stronger cattle did conceive, that Jacob laid the rods before the eyes of the cattle in the gutters, that they might conceive among the rods.

⁴² But when the cattle were feeble, he put them not in: so the feebler were Laban's, and the stronger Jacob's.

⁴³ And the man increased exceedingly, and had much cattle, and maidservants, and menservants, and camels, and asses.

Genesis 30:27-43

I wondered why Jacob chose to create an image in the mind of these animals at the time of conception. Conception time is one of the most critical times in the life of a living thing because the image you hold in your heart and mind during conception is usually imprinted on the life of the seed that is conceived.

The grace to write was not something I was actively pursing. It was deposited through a spiritual experience with God. I never had a dream of being an author and not as quickly as I did. The proliferation I am experiencing in writing did not come like a lightning bolt from heaven. It is proliferation based on knowledge. I created a shelf in my bedroom and lined it with books from some chosen authors, so every time a manuscript is being worked on, I place it between the works of these authors in a specific order and prophesy that the same grace on the material from these authors rest on our books.

Suddenly, every time a material was being worked on, supernatural outbursts of insight started to hit my spirit at such speeds that I could hardly cope. These were not things I read in the books of the authors rather they were things I discovered in my search for knowledge. Contents of books came as though the valve on a high pressure water store had just been opened. Since I caught this revelation, I have never struggled for material. The minute I start typing, my mind just becomes like the pen of a ready writer.

Innovation gives you the presence of mind to be able to create something out of nothing. You become productive in the most challenging circumstances of life.

The Insight of Joseph

Insight is the ability to draw conclusions from facts regarding a course of action. These conclusions are usually very simple and easily understood by all. In these days, we could call it *reading through the lines or acumen*. This is the ability to intuitively understand the true nature of a thing. Insight is the vehicle that God uses to preserve the future for believers. With insight, we can start the process of creating tomorrow's solutions today.

In the world of business, companies pay top dollar for those who have excellent business acumen. What they are really saying is that we need someone in our business who can look at the facts about our organisation and advice us on a way to go that will mean when problems arrive in future we already have a solution. Such companies are always steps ahead of the game.

Too many people wait for problems to occur then look for solutions. Even God demonstrated this insight. I wonder why He offered up Christ before the foundation of the world (*1 Peter 1:19-20*). He(God) offered Him(Jesus) before the foundation of the world, which was before Adam. Did God expect Adam was going to fall? No. Did God expect Jesus to manifest whether Adam fell or not. I believe He did (*Genesis 3:22-24*).

Both Noah and Joseph had the knowledge to deliver solutions before the problems arose because the knowledge of God had been in their hearts.

The insight of Joseph was twofold. One he knew what the dreams of Pharaoh meant and secondly he knew what needed to be done in preparation for the events the dreams foretold. As believers, we should be interpreting issues of national importance. This story also shows us that God can speak to whosoever He chooses.

> [25] And Joseph said unto Pharaoh, The dream of Pharaoh is one: God hath shewed Pharaoh what he is about to do.
> [26] The seven good kine are seven years; and the seven good ears are seven years: the dream is one.
> [27] And the seven thin and ill favoured kine that came up after them are seven years; and the seven empty ears blasted with the east wind shall be seven years of famine.
> [28] This is the thing which I have spoken unto Pharaoh: What God is about to do he sheweth unto Pharaoh.
> [29] Behold, there come seven years of great plenty throughout all the land of Egypt:
> [30] And there shall arise after them seven years of famine; and all the plenty shall be forgotten in the land of Egypt; and the famine shall consume the land;
> [31] And the plenty shall not be known in the land by reason of that famine following; for it shall be very grievous.
> [32] And for that the dream was doubled unto Pharaoh twice; it is because the thing is established by God, and God will shortly bring it to pass.
> [33] Now therefore let Pharaoh look out a man discreet and wise, and set him over the land of Egypt.
> [34] Let Pharaoh do this, and let him appoint officers over the land, and take up the fifth part of the land of Egypt in the seven plenteous years.
> [35] And let them gather all the food of those good years that come, and lay up corn under the hand of Pharaoh, and let them keep food in the cities.
> [36] And that food shall be for store to the land against the seven years of famine, which shall be in the land of Egypt; that the land perish not through the famine.
> [37] And the thing was good in the eyes of Pharaoh, and in the eyes of all his servants.
> [38] And Pharaoh said unto his servants, Can we find such a one as this is, a man in whom the Spirit of God is?
> [39] And Pharaoh said unto Joseph, Forasmuch as God hath shewed thee all this, there is none so discreet and wise as thou art:
>
> *Genesis 41:25-39*

There are multiple dreams God has placed in the minds of presidents, governors, prime-ministers, company leaders and rulers in authority and all that remains is for believers to start interpreting dreams while in their prison experiences of life. Your door to greatness may be found in the person you help while in your prison of life experience. Do not be too self focused that you miss this exit opportunity.

One thing common to both Noah and Joseph is that there was no precedence on the scale of the task that was placed before them. The force of life in them produced results when there was a demand on it. There is nothing mystical about this. In fact, I believe it is easier to operate in insight by the Holy Spirit than it is to seek help from a "wise man or magician" of this time. I always wonder why these so called wise men always seem deprived themselves and lacking power when faced with real issues. Look at the how Daniel was described in by king Bel-shaz'-zar

> [11] There is a man in thy kingdom, in whom is the spirit of the holy gods; and in the days of thy father light and understanding and wisdom, like the wisdom of the gods, was found in him; whom the king Nebuchadnezzar thy father, the king, I say, thy father, made master of the magicians, astrologers, Chaldeans, and soothsayers;
> [12] Forasmuch as an excellent spirit, and knowledge, and understanding, interpreting of dreams, and shewing of hard sentences, and dissolving of doubts, were found in the same Daniel, whom the king named Belteshazzar: now let Daniel be called, and he will shew the interpretation.
> [13] Then was Daniel brought in before the king. And the king spake and said unto Daniel, Art thou that Daniel, which art of the children of the captivity of Judah, whom the king my father brought out of Jewry?
> [14] I have even heard of thee, that the spirit of the gods is in thee, and that light and understanding and excellent wisdom is found in thee.
> [15] And now the wise men, the astrologers, have been brought in before me, that they should read this writing, and make known unto me the interpretation thereof: but they could not shew the interpretation of

the thing:
¹⁶ And I have heard of thee, that thou canst make interpretations, and dissolve doubts: now if thou canst read the writing, and make known to me the interpretation thereof, thou shalt be clothed with scarlet, and have a chain of gold about thy neck, and shalt be the third ruler in the kingdom.
¹⁷ Then Daniel answered and said before the king, Let thy gifts be to thyself, and give thy rewards to another; yet I will read the writing unto the king, and make known to him the interpretation.

Daniel 5:11-17

Daniel was interpreting dreams, dissolving doubts, showing hard sentences. Daniel was able to draw conclusions from the facts but notice the wise men and astrologers could not do it. God is always greater than man under any circumstance. It is easy to use insight for material gain but notice Daniel rejected the offer. Why? His God was more than able to meet his needs. I wonder what life would be like if people's needs are not only met from the works of their hands but also by the proclamation of words from their mouth. I remember in 2009 when the Lord spoke to me after I had sacrificed something significant for Him. He said, *"Now it is time for your needs to be met by the proclamation of words of faith from your mouth and not just the works of your hands. The same way no man can discover how the ram showed up for Abraham, no man will be able to discover your source of wealth."*

After this, money started to show up in ways that beat my imagination. People heard of what God was doing and just wanted to support us. This is not license not to work. It is license to enter into the fullness of work. I once said to my wife, *"If your salary stops coming from your employer, maybe you have stopped working for them"* In the same way, if the supernatural in not breaking forth in your life, maybe you have stopped working for God, your life employer.

The Inventions of Uzziah

The scale and impact of inventions do not seem to be on the same level as it used to be. Where are the Thomas Edisons and the Isaac Newtons of our days? While inventors continue to invent, where are the inventions on the level of the discoveries of electricity and the theories of relativity? What we must not forget is that the physical inventions we see are products in themselves. The real driver in inventions is *"intellectual inventions"*. It is men pushing the mind to its limits. Before every ground breaking idea became a reality, there was a revolution in the mind. This is one of the greatest times to be alive. The challenges today present more opportunities than can be exhausted in your lifetime.

Whatever you see anyone achieve without God, be reassured, you can achieve greater heights with God. One of the early stories of inventions we read about in the Bible is that of the Tower of Babel.

> ¹*And the whole earth was of one language, and of one speech.*
> ²*And it came to pass, as they journeyed from the east, that they found a plain in the land of Shinar; and they dwelt there.*
> ³*And they said one to another, Go to, let us make brick, and burn them thoroughly. And they had brick for stone, and slime had they for morter.*
> ⁴*And they said, Go to, let us build us a city and a tower, whose top may reach unto heaven; and let us make us a name, lest we be scattered abroad upon the face of the whole earth.*
> ⁵*And the LORD came down to see the city and the tower, which the children of men builded.*
> ⁶*And the LORD said, Behold, the people is one, and they have all one language; and this they begin to do: and now nothing will be restrained from them, which they have imagined to do.*
>
> *Genesis 11:1-6*

This demonstrates the unlimited capacity of the mind to

conceive and create what is conceived. Even though this was after Noah, the concept of building a tower whose top may reach unto heaven was not such a bad thought and they believed in the possibility of achieving their dream (*Genesis 11:5*). I wonder what the architectural drawings would have looked like or maybe they had none. How complex would the foundation have been? One thing we are sure of is that they had four key elements going for them. Firstly, the people were one, signifying unity. Secondly, they had one language or means of communicating and interacting with themselves. Thirdly they had imagination and lastly, they were not procrastinators. They got busy immediately. Inventors get to work quickly. They are not afraid of failing and they consider failures as necessary steps in the journey of discoveries.

Looking through the biographies of some great inventors in history, we realise that a number of them had God as a strong anchor in their lives and God gave them discoveries they did not expect but anticipated.

> ¹*Then all the people of Judah took Uzziah, who was sixteen years old, and made him king in the room of his father Amaziah.*
> ²*He built Eloth, and restored it to Judah, after that the king slept with his fathers.*
> ³*Sixteen years old was Uzziah when he began to reign, and he reigned fifty and two years in Jerusalem. His mother's name also was Jecoliah of Jerusalem.*
> ⁴*And he did that which was right in the sight of the LORD, according to all that his father Amaziah did.*
> ⁵*And he sought God in the days of Zechariah, who had understanding in the visions of God: and as long as he sought the LORD, God made him to prosper.*
>
> *2 Chronicles 26:1-5*

One of the important factors in the life of Uzziah is that he sought God in the days of a prophet who had understanding in the visions of God. These same type of prophets exist in the Church today (*Ephesians 4:11-15*). Find them out, that you may prosper. Remember that in the Old Testament, while Elijah was a prophet well known, there were seven thousand others prophets whom God recognised who even Elijah knew nothing about. For every Elijah or Elisha you know, there may be another seven thousand not too far away. Do not despise them.

As long as Uzziah sought God, he prospered.

> *⁸And the Ammonites gave gifts to Uzziah: and his name spread abroad even to the entering in of Egypt; for he strengthened himself exceedingly.*
> *⁹Moreover Uzziah built towers in Jerusalem at the corner gate, and at the valley gate, and at the turning of the wall, and fortified them.*
> *¹⁰Also he built towers in the desert, and digged many wells: for he had much cattle, both in the low country, and in the plains: husbandmen also, and vine dressers in the mountains, and in Carmel: for he loved husbandry.*
> *¹¹Moreover Uzziah had an host of fighting men, that went out to war by bands, according to the number of their account by the hand of Jeiel the scribe and Maaseiah the ruler, under the hand of Hananiah, one of the king's captains.*
> *¹²The whole number of the chief of the fathers of the mighty men of valour were two thousand and six hundred.*
> *¹³And under their hand was an army, three hundred thousand and seven thousand and five hundred, that made war with mighty power, to help the king against the enemy.*
> *¹⁴And Uzziah prepared for them throughout all the host shields, and spears, and helmets, and habergeons, and bows, and slings to cast stones.*
> *¹⁵AND HE MADE IN JERUSALEM ENGINES, INVENTED BY CUNNING MEN, TO BE ON THE TOWERS AND UPON THE BULWARKS, TO SHOOT ARROWS AND GREAT STONES WITHAL. AND HIS NAME SPREAD FAR ABROAD; FOR HE WAS MARVELLOUSLY HELPED, TILL HE WAS STRONG.*
>
> 2 Chronicles 26:8-15

Uzziah made advanced weapons through the inventions of cunning men. Why was he able to make these things work? The Bible says he was *marvellously helped till he was strong.*

Inventions require help, it is not a *"star-man"* assignment. You cannot work inventions on your own. Inventions are made standing on the shoulders of others. It is the demonstration of a collection of minds working on a common goal. Inventions are not to build a name for yourself. Inventions are God working through you to solve the problems the devil has caused humanity.

I believe there is a strong wave of inventions going to enter the world through the Church. Christians will be seen as the gods they are. Gradually, the lies of the Devil will be pushed back and we will walk in realms of possibilities we never imagined.

Chapter Key Points

Your door to greatness may be found in the person you help while in your prison of life experience. Do not be too self focused that you miss this exit opportunity

What is chance but an opportunity for which you were prepared. When preparation meets chance, elevation is inevitable

"If your salary stops coming from your employer, maybe you have stopped working for them" In the same way, if the supernatural in not breaking forth in your life, maybe you have stopped working for God, your life employer

Inventions are made standing on the shoulders of others. It is the demonstration of a collection of minds working on a common goal

www.ingramcontent.com/pod-product-compliance
Lightning Source LLC
LaVergne TN
LVHW091308080426
835510LV00007B/412